Contemporary Issues in Mediation

Volume 6

Related Titles by the Author

Contemporary Issues in Mediation Volume 1
ISBN: 978-981-3108-35-6
ISBN: 978-981-3108-36-3 (pbk)

Contemporary Issues in Mediation Volume 2
ISBN: 978-981-3225-63-3
ISBN: 978-981-3225-64-0 (pbk)

Contemporary Issues in Mediation Volume 3
ISBN: 978-981-3270-81-7
ISBN: 978-981-3271-76-0 (pbk)

Contemporary Issues in Mediation Volume 4
ISBN: 978-981-120-911-6
ISBN: 978-981-120-928-4 (pbk)

Contemporary Issues in Mediation Volume 5
ISBN: 978-981-122-052-4
ISBN: 978-981-122-109-5 (pbk)

Contemporary Issues in Mediation

Volume 6

Joel Lee
Singapore International Mediation Institute, Singapore
Faculty of Law, National University of Singapore

Marcus Lim
Lupl. Singapore

with Isabella Tan
Singapore International Mediation Institute, Singapore

Guest Editor: Alvin Cheng
School of Law, Singapore University of Social Sciences

simi
SINGAPORE INTERNATIONAL MEDIATION INSTITUTE

World Scientific

Published by

World Scientific Publishing Co. Pte. Ltd.
5 Toh Tuck Link, Singapore 596224
USA office: 27 Warren Street, Suite 401-402, Hackensack, NJ 07601
UK office: 57 Shelton Street, Covent Garden, London WC2H 9HE

Library of Congress Cataloging-in-Publication Data
Names: Lee, Joel, editor. | Lim, Marcus, editor.
Title: Contemporary issues in mediation (v. 1) / Edited by Joel Lee
(Singapore International Mediation Institute, Singapore),
Marcus Lim (Singapore International Mediation Institute, Singapore).
Description: Hackensack, New Jersey : World Scientific, 2016.
Identifiers: LCCN 2016004240| ISBN 9789813108356 (hardcover : alk. paper) |
ISBN 9789813108363 (pbk.)
Subjects: LCSH: Dispute resolution (Law) | Mediation. | Dispute resolution (Law)--Singapore. | Mediation--Singapore.
Classification: LCC K2390 .C667 2016 | DDC 347/.09--dc23
LC record available at http://lccn.loc.gov/2016004240

Contemporary issues in mediation (v. 6)
ISBN 978-981-124-142-0

British Library Cataloguing-in-Publication Data
A catalogue record for this book is available from the British Library.

For any available supplementary material, please visit
https://www.worldscientific.com/worldscibooks/10.1142/12400#t=suppl

Typeset by Stallion Press
Email: enquiries@stallionpress.com

These essays are another demonstration of Singapore's leadership in the development and use of mediation in the Asia-Pacific region, exemplified by the Singapore Convention on Mediation. They also highlight the worldwide need for comprehensive, compulsory training in the skills of negotiation, mediation and mediation advocacy, particularly in university law schools, as well as the potentially permanent transition from face-to-face to online methods of conducting and participating in mediation brought about by the current pandemic and the technological advances that have taken place over the last four decades. The authors are to be congratulated for their insights and efforts, as are the editors for their professionalism.

Alan L Limbury
Negotiator, Arbitrator and Accredited Mediator
Managing Director, Strategic Resolution Australia

The eclectic collection of essays ranges from specific issues during the mediation process (e.g. confidentiality) to reflections on appropriate mediation styles, to larger issues such as whether mediation is the appropriate dispute resolution mechanism for certain types of disputes. Volume 6 will serve as a useful reference point on the importance of human presence and the necessity of humans as mediators in the future with essays that explore the introduction of technology in online mediation and artificial intelligence. Congratulations to the editors for a thoughtful collection of essays that allows the reader to reflect on the present and ponder the future.

Low Lih Jeng
Senior Consultant, Sage Mediation
Former District Judge, State Courts of Singapore

Contents

Foreword for the Series

By William Ury

A young man was hiking through the woods. He came to a clearing and sat on a rock to rest. As he ate his lunch, he noticed an old man moving through the clearing in a very deliberate way. The man would walk a specific number of steps, poke a hole in the ground with his walking stick, drop something in and then repeat the process. Curious, the young man approached the old man and asked him what he was doing.

> *The old man replied, "Well, I'm planting trees."*
> *"But why?" the young man asked.*
> *"When I was younger," the old man said, "this entire land was filled with trees. But over time, many trees had been cut down. I come here every day to plant trees."*
> *Fascinated, the young man asked, "How long have you been doing this?"*
> *"Forty years." was the matter of fact reply.*
> *"Forty years!" exclaimed the young man.*
> *"Yup," the old man replied. Gesturing to a grove of young trees in the distance, he said with some pride, "I planted those 10 years ago."*
> *The young man was incredulous. "That's great but these trees will take a long time to grow! And, if you will pardon me saying so, you may not live long enough to see the seeds you are planting today grow into trees!"*
> *"This is true," said the old man "I have lived long enough to see some of the fruits of my labour. But the seeds I plant today are not for me, but for you."*

It has now been just about 40 years since I had the privilege of embarking on the adventure of teaching and practicing in the field of negotiation and mediation. During that time, I have had the joy of learning from and working with many highly talented and skilled individuals in academia, law, business and diplomacy. In those early days, there was very little scholarly writing in this area. After all, the field was relatively new and viewed by many with caution, if not outright skepticism.

Over the years, I have been gratified to watch the field of mediation grow considerably. Today, practitioners, teachers and researchers can be found in every part of the world. The teaching, practice and scholarship of negotiation and mediation constitute a dynamic system in which each contributes to the others. New tools and frameworks have been developed as a result of research, taught to practitioners, and then tested and refined in the field, which in turn has informed further research. This interplay between theory and practice has been vital in developing new insights and methods.

Yet the field of negotiation and mediation is still young. As we look back on the progress, we might be satisfied with the seeds we have planted which have sprouted into trees. Yet, as the concepts and practices spread around the world, we have a responsibility to ensure that future generations will be able to build on all that has been achieved. We must continue to plant seeds, not for ourselves, but for those to come.

This is why this book project by the Singapore International Mediation Institute is such a timely endeavour worthy of support. It is said that a journey of a thousand miles begins with a single step. The Singapore International Mediation Institute is taking that first step to inspire the youth of today and encourage them to engage in scholarship about mediation. It provides them the platform and the opportunity to plant seeds for the benefit and enjoyment of future generations.

As the first of its kind in Singapore, I look forward to seeing this book series not only continue to flourish, but also to show the way forward through innovative and thought-provoking work.

And I take this opportunity to wish you much success in getting to yes!

William Ury
Co-founder, Harvard Negotiation Project
Co-author, *Getting to Yes*
31 May 2016

About the Guest Editor

Alvin Cheng

Alvin Cheng is a Senior Lecturer at the Singapore University of Social Sciences (School of Law) and a Consultant with Aequitas Law LLP. He has been in private legal practice for over 25 years — mainly in litigation and dispute resolution. A graduate of the University of London, Alvin has been called to the Bar of England and Wales, and the Singapore Bar.

Alvin is a mediator with the Singapore Mediation Centre (SMC), the State Courts Centre for Dispute Resolution and the Law Society Mediation Scheme. He is also a member of SMC's panel of Collaborative Family Practitioners.

He is an accredited mediator with the Regent's University London (School of Psychotherapy and Psychology), and he has received advanced training from Conflict Coaching International and the Strauss Institute for Dispute Resolution (Pepperdine University School of Law).

Alvin is a member of SMC's Adjunct Training Faculty and has trained professionals from both private and public sectors, including community leaders, foreign dignitaries and judges. He is also a teaching fellow of the Singapore Institute of Legal Education, where he teaches mediation advocacy skills.

Alvin is a founding member of the Society of Mediation Professionals (Singapore) and he has served on its Executive Committee as Honorary Secretary and Honorary Treasurer.

About the Editors

Joel Lee

Joel Lee is a Professor at the Faculty of Law, the National University of Singapore. Joel co-pioneered the teaching of Negotiation and Mediation in the Singapore Universities and has played a significant role in furthering the development of mediation in Singapore, not just in education but in practice. A graduate of Victoria University of Wellington and Harvard Law Schools, Joel is a partner with CMP Cambridge (USA) and a principal mediator with the Singapore Mediation Centre.

Joel was a member of the International Mediation Institute's Independent Standards Commission and Intercultural Taskforce and was also a key member of the Ministry of Law's Working Group on International Commercial Mediation. Joel is presently the founding Chair of the Board of the Singapore International Mediation Institute. He is also a Certified Trainer of Neuro-Linguistic Programming (NLP).

Joel has taught overseas at the University of Copenhagen (Denmark), University of Law, Economics and Science of Aix-Marseille (Aix-en-Provence France) and Anglia Law School (UK) and is the co-editor and co-author of *An Asian Perspective on Mediation* and the *Singapore Mediation Handbook*, and the General Editor for the *Asian Journal on Mediation*. In 2011, Joel was awarded the Outstanding Educator Award which is the National University of Singapore's highest teaching award.

Marcus Lim

Marcus Lim is the Country Manager (Singapore) for Lupl the open industry platform for legal matters that brings together in one place the people, conversations, documents, data and knowledge for legal matters, providing real-time 360-degree visibility and control.

Prior to joining Lupl, Marcus was the first Executive Director and later, CEO, of the Singapore International Mediation Institute, where he spearheaded many initiatives in growing the organisation into an internationally recognised and credible brand for mediation standards.

He holds appointments as a Lecturer for the Negotiation and Mediation Workshops at the Faculty of Law, the National University of Singapore, and was the coordinator for both courses in 2017. A graduate from the prestigious Law and Business Double Degree programme at the National University of Singapore, he is a consultant with CMP Cambridge (USA). He is certified in the Thomas-Kilmann Instrument for Conflict and Change Management. Marcus is a SIMI Certified Mediator, an Associate Mediator with the Singapore Mediation Centre, and a court-appointed volunteer mediator for the Small Claims Tribunal at the State Courts.

Marcus has extensive experience conducting negotiation and mediation trainings for staff and management of government organisations, as well as multinational corporations across a diverse range of sectors, such as finance, retail, real estate, IT, education and the healthcare industry.

Editors' Note

The year 2020, in many ways, was a momentous one thanks to the Covid-19 pandemic. Governments, companies, and people had to adapt quickly, finding new ways to communicate and confer. Online video conferencing tools became the "bread-and-butter" of everyday business and the mediation sphere is no exception. Online mediation has become and continues to be a trend, well into 2021.

This volume of Contemporary Issues in Mediation (CIIM) is important. It marks the transition between two worlds — one where in-person and cross-border mediations could occur and one where technology *rules*. At the point of publishing, it would also have been almost a year since the Singapore Convention on Mediation has entered into force. In the six years since the first volume of CIIM was published, we are excited to see the growing diversity of entries from keen students all over the world and the increasing depth of the issues discussed.

CIIM Volume 6 is full of fascinating, forward-thinking interdisciplinary insights regarding the multi-faceted role of mediation in our world today. Our top entry, "The Need for Mediation Advocacy Standards in Singapore", by Levin Lin Lok Yan, evaluates the need for professional standards for mediation advocates and presents a list of proposals for consideration. This is particularly enterprising as Singapore continues to push the frontiers of international alternative, or rather amicable dispute resolution. Our runner-up entry, "Decoding the B.S. (Behavioural Science) in Mediation", by Utsav Rakshit, adopts a different tone. His well-illustrated piece touches on cognitive biases and what to do about them in the context of mediation. Our wide selection of topics, ranging from religion (Sabrina Chau Shu Ning), domestic violence (Tomoyuki

Lewis Ban), finance (Terence Yeo) to artificial intelligence (Chloe Chua Kay Ee), is sure to make this volume a real page-turner.

As always, this publication would not have been possible without the support and effort of many people. We would like to take this opportunity to express our heartfelt thanks to:

- Our wonderful, better halves, Pearl, Li Jing and Suyin, for their unending patience and love;
- Ms Isabella Tan, for her dedicated and invaluable professional assistance to the editorial team;
- Mr William Ury, for writing the foreword for the series;
- Members of SIMI's board, past and present for their unwavering support of the project (Ms Josephine Hadikusumo, Mr Calvin Phua, Professor Nadja Alexander, Poon Hong Yuen, Mr Han Kok Juan, Mr Michael Leathes and Ms Irena Vanenkova);
- The Singapore Ministry of Law, for continuing to support our work;
- The National University of Singapore, Faculty of Law, for being a stalwart supporter of SIMI's operations;
- Our publishers, the World Scientific Publishing Company for their patience and guidance in bringing another volume to publication; and
- Our students (past and present) from the National University of Singapore, Faculty of Law and Singapore Management University School of Law, as well as all over the world, for always being an inspiration to our work.

Last but not least, we would like to thank you, the reader, for supporting SIMI and this book. We hope that this project continues to inspire you in your work, whatever field it may be, to find collaborative solutions in resolving your disputes.

Joel Lee, Marcus Lim and Alvin Cheng
Singapore
22 June 2021

About the CIIM Essay Competition

As part of SIMI's (Singapore International Mediation Institute) mission to promote awareness and interest in mediation, SIMI regularly organises an essay competition to help promote mediation academia among undergraduates and students in tertiary institutions. Submissions are welcome from students not only pursuing studies in law but also other disciplines. Selected entries will be featured in an annual edition of the *Contemporary Issues in Mediation*, with attractive prizes for some of the best submissions.

About SIMI

The Singapore International Mediation Institute (SIMI) was incorporated on 15 July 2014 as a non-profit organisation supported by the Ministry of Law. SIMI is a subsidiary of the National University of Singapore (NUS) and is housed at the NUS Faculty of Law.

SIMI is headed by an international Board of Directors with representatives from both mediation practitioners as well as corporate users of mediation, to further its mission to (1) set and achieve high mediation standards through the professionalisation of mediation; (2) promote understanding and inspire the use of mediation; (3) stimulate and facilitate the development and growth of mediation through research and innovation; and (4) foster a strong mediation community in Asia by engaging stakeholders in discussion, events and outreach activities.

The Need for Mediation Advocacy Standards in Singapore

Levin Lin Lok Yan

I. Introduction

The Singapore Convention on Mediation ("SCM") was signed by 46 states on 7 August 2019 when it was first opened for signing. As of April 2020, 51 states have signed it. The SCM has been ratified by three states[a] and entered into force on 12 September 2020. The SCM Signing Ceremony and Conference was hosted by Singapore, signifying Singapore's involvement in the global development of mediation as a dispute settlement process. This contributes to strengthening Singapore's position as a leading dispute resolution hub.[1] The SCM aims to facilitate international trade and promote mediation as an effective method of resolving trade dispute by establishing a legal framework to invoke and enforce mediated settlement agreements across borders.[2] The Singapore Parliament passed the Singapore Convention on Mediation Bill ("Bill") on 6 January 2020 to implement Singapore's obligations under the SCM.[3]

With the growth of mediation in Singapore, it begs the question whether there are any gaps that need to be filled. Professional standards for mediators have led to a growing pool of qualified mediators in Singapore. Yet, there is little or no progress for mediation advocates. Mediation consists of a neutral third-party — the mediator — and parties who are seeking to resolve their dispute(s), represented by their lawyers.

[a]As of June 2021, the SCM has been ratified by six states.

What is the role of a lawyer in mediation? Lawyers are there to advise their clients and to contribute to the mediation in a collaborative and constructive manner. This helps their clients to achieve a resolution that reflects their interests and needs. With representation, parties are able have an informed negotiation, facilitating the mediation process. In many jurisdictions,[4] as in Singapore, mediation is becoming or is already a standard feature in dispute resolution. With court-mandated mediation, lawyers are increasingly engaged in mediation as well. Given the contributions that a lawyer can make to mediation, the importance of a mediation advocate cannot be overlooked. Yet, glaringly, Singapore has no mediation advocate standards nor any mandatory training programme in place.

This chapter seeks to analyse the need for a mediation advocacy standard in Singapore and where we can turn to for guidance. This chapter will first highlight the mediation trends in Singapore that have led to an increase in mediation cases. With that, there will be an analysis of the specific mindset required for mediation advocacy and how it differs from the mindset many lawyers have going into practice. Considering the skillset required, this chapter will point out how current education and training that is available in Singapore is insufficient. Consequently, this chapter will consider international or regional standards that are in place and how Singapore can take guidance from there.

II. Mediation trends in Singapore

Mediation as a dispute resolution process has gained traction over the years. This can be seen in the Singapore State Courts' attitude towards introducing mediation as a form of alternative dispute resolution ("ADR"). The Practice Direction No. 2 of 2012[5] first introduced a presumption of ADR which provides for automatic referral of all civil cases for ADR, making it the first stop of a court process[6] in adopting a "more holistic mode of advocacy".[7] Subsequently, ADR was termed as "Court Dispute Resolution" ("CDR") in Practice Direction No. 3 of 2017.[8] This reflected another shift in the Singapore judiciary's attitude towards mediation. Mediation is no longer an *alternative*, instead it is a significant first stop court process. The current State Courts Practice Direction encourages parties to consider non-adversarial ways of resolving their disputes before turning to litigation as a last resort. Mediation has also been included in the court processes of the Family Justice Courts ("FCJ"). The FCJ may direct parties to attend mediation, encouraging parties to resolve their matters amicably.[9] Family proceedings involving a child under the age of 21 are mandated to go for mediation.[10] The introduction of mediation into Singapore's courts has no doubt led to an increase in the use of mediation. Furthermore, it is now the professional duty of advocates and solicitors to advise their clients about the different ways their disputes may be resolved using an appropriate form of ADR.[11] This is supported by guidelines furnished by the Supreme Court, whereby lawyers have a duty to explain the advantages of mediation, the process and what might be achieved over and above what remedies are available through the courts.[12] As the Supreme Court guidelines also apply to civil and commercial claims above S$250,000 which are dealt with by the High Court, this signals that all disputes regardless of their nature or amount involved, are capable of resolution through mediation as long as the parties are willing.

Apart from court mediation, private mediations have been administered at the Singapore Mediation Centre (SMC) and the Singapore International Mediation Centre (SIMC). The two centres were created to encourage the provision of mediation services.[13] The SMC has handled civil cases where disputed amounts go up to S$1.06 billion with 60% of such cases initiated directly by parties.[14] The SIMC has also administered international mediation claims of up to S$600 million from 20 jurisdictions.[15] This illustrates the growing presence of Singapore on the world map as a hub for mediation. These efforts culminated in the establishment of the Singapore International Mediation Institute (SIMI) that enforces the national mediation standard. With a robust accreditation system, SIMI has promoted the growth of both national and international mediators in Singapore. With these institutions in place, a national mediation advocacy standard will allow for mediation to continue developing and making its mark as an attractive dispute resolution process. Such a standard will uphold the legitimacy and effectiveness of the mediation process, thereby increasing the demand for mediation cases, both domestic and international.

III. Mediation advocacy — a skillset

Mediation advocacy is different from trial advocacy because the objectives of mediation and litigation are different. Figure 1 illustrates the differences succinctly:

Mediation	Litigation
Joint problem solving	Adversarial focus
Focus on future solutions	Determining fault based on the past
Deals with legal and non-legal issues	Deals only with legal issues
Advocate needs to persuade ALL parties	Advocate needs to only persuade the Judge
Advocate has to work together with the Neutral	Neutral only has to be persuaded

Figure 1. Comparing mediation and litigation.[16]

Accordingly, lawyers need to be trained to be skilled mediation advocates. For lawyers to contribute during a mediation, a multi-dimensional mindset shift is necessary. This includes a shift from:

(a) the adversarial to **collaborative**;
(b) win-lose to **win-win**;
(c) a past focus to **future focus**;
(d) a focus on lawyers in the trial process to **a focus on the parties in the mediation process**; and
(e) the need to convince a third-party umpire to **the need to reach a consensus with the other side in relation to the resolution of the dispute.**[17]

(a) Adversarial to collaborative

Singapore has inherited an adversarial system where "parties were left to control the pace and progress of the proceedings".[18] This has shaped lawyers' minds to prepare for battle, whether in the courtroom or not, to secure a win *over the other party*. This mindset, unsurprisingly, is detrimental to mediation. Preparing or entering a mediation with this mindset would undermine the process and outcome of the mediation. Mediation requires lawyers to move towards collaborative problem-solving with the assistance of the mediator.[19]

Collaborative problem-solving requires trust. A mediation advocate needs to be able to listen actively and share information strategically. Yet trust is something that is sorely lacking in the litigation process. This change in mindset is at odds with the existing legal education that lawyers receive. Thus, a lawyer going for mediation will need training and practice to be a mediation advocate.

(b) Win-lose to win-win

Closely tied to a collaborative attitude is a win-win mindset. This is described as a "frame of mind and heart that constantly seeks mutual benefit in all human interactions".[20] In the predominant approach to settling cases, the results are almost always a win-lose and sometimes, even a lose-lose for clients. Whereas in mediation, the process seeks to arrive at a resolution that is mutually beneficial and satisfactory to both parties.[21]

(c) A past focus to a future focus

The nature and process of litigation brings to the forefront the cause of the dispute, focusing on what has happened supported by evidence and how the other party can compensate for it. Conversely, in mediation, parties are encouraged to focus on how they want to move forward and to brainstorm options that can help address what has happened without attributing blame. There is little to no hint of "punishing" someone for the alleged "injustice" or "inconvenience". Instead, parties are assisted to recognise the value in working towards a solution that would end the problem and hopefully build a future relationship.

(d) Focusing on parties during mediation

During trial, the focus is on the lawyers instead of parties. Lawyers present their legal arguments trying to persuade the bench, parties are rarely present, and their personal concerns are irrelevant. In contrast, mediation advocates are there to represent their client's interests and concerns to the other party and the mediator, wanting to reach a resolution. Parties are often present and do participate throughout the course of the mediation. The process is party-focused and hence, legal arguments take a backseat while lawyers advance their client's interests.

(e) The need to reach a consensus with the other side

This underpins the collaborative attitude of a mediation advocate — it is only possible to arrive at a resolution when there is consensus. Trying to reach a consensus is hardly something a lawyer does during trial. Instead, it is a matter of persuading the court of who deserves to win. In mediation, this consensus is not merely achieved through positional bargaining, but through careful and interest-based negotiation where the outcome is mutually satisfying, thereby leading to a greater likelihood of implementation.

Such a complex shift towards the skills and attitudes required is foreign to both corporate and trial lawyers. Having a lawyer approach mediation like it is a trial will only cause the mediation process to break down. In a worst-case scenario, a lawyer who does not believe in the mediation process (because of the lack of training), tries sabotaging the mediation so that the matter can proceed to trial (where he/she feels more comfortable fighting at). This will result in the client's dissatisfactory experience with mediation and thus, being averse to it in the future. It is necessary that education and training are implemented in accordance to a national standard, to cultivate a pool of mediation advocates as more disputes turn to mediation for resolution.

IV. Lack of training available in Singapore

In light of the skills that need to be taught and attributes that need to be inculcated, the current legal education system in Singapore is insufficient for building a pool of mediation advocates. Furthermore, there are no standards in place offering guidance to lawyers on how to be a mediation advocate nor regulating organisations that are carrying out mediation advocacy workshops. Currently, the only education or training on mediation that lawyers receive are optional courses in law school and the Singapore Bar Examinations.

A. *Learning from professional mediator standards in Singapore*

There are numerous workshops on being a mediator by organisations verified by SIMI's Qualifying Assessment Program ("QAPs"). SIMI does so by certifying the competency of mediators, applying and enforcing standards of professional ethics and requiring continuing professional development for SIMI accredited mediators.[22] As a result, there is consistency in the mediator trainings that are carried out by different organisations, ensuring a standard of professionalism and contributing to the growth of mediators in Singapore. On top of these, having a standard implemented by an independent body would allow for regular review of the standards and processes in place.

As SIMI has done for mediator standards, the same can and should be done for mediation advocacy. Such a professional standards body will set the foundation of skilled mediation advocacy in Singapore. Training can be done by SIMI's QAPs where trained mediation advocates will receive accreditation. With training carried out based on a professional standard, this will ensure (i) that lawyers are able to maximise their roles in mediation, (ii) mediation remains a legitimate form of dispute resolution and (iii) continuous development of mediation in Singapore's legal system and amongst international commercial disputes. Furthermore, it signals to the world that Singapore is taking the lead in mediation advocacy, establishing the highest of mediation standards. This may result in more international commercial cases being resolved in Singapore.

Apart from professionalism, having a standards body also ensures the enforcement of a Code of Ethics that is specifically applicable to mediation advocates. This adds to the legitimacy of mediation as a dispute resolution process, clarifying any inconsistencies or gaps in the present Legal Profession (Professional Conduct) Rules.[23] Such a development will build the public's trust in mediation and thus, promote mediation domestically as well.

(1) *International Mediation Institute*

A key institution that has contributed to international mediation advocacy standards is the International Mediation Institute (IMI). The IMI has a set of Competency Criteria for Mediation Advocates/Advisors[24] ("Criteria") which we can take guidance from. This seeks to establish a professional and technical basis for enabling disputing parties to identify experienced professionals to advise and represent them at mediation. The Criteria consists of two broad categories: (i) General Requirements for Mediation Advocacy and (ii) Substantive Criteria for Mediation Advocates/Advisors. This sets out an extensive list governing standards such as methodology and transparency. The criteria is intended to offer guidance to IMI's QAPs in planning their training program and assessments. However, such a list has its drawbacks as it might result in practical difficulties in implementation, not to mention overlapping requirements.

(2) *European Union Mediation Development Toolkit*

The European Commission for the Efficiency of Justice ("CEPEJ") has developed a training programme for lawyers to assist clients in mediation under the Mediation Development Toolkit.[25] The training programme was developed to provide lawyers with the tools and techniques required to successfully assist clients throughout the process of mediation. The programme consists of three distinctive parts: (i) principles, ethics and conflict management; (ii) the mediation process and the role of the accompanying lawyer; and (iii) the proper use of mediation.

Although the programme operates at a regional level, the approach taken by the European Union is worthy of mirroring. Despite its implementation at a regional level, the approach taken by the European Union focuses on training lawyers to be equipped to assist their clients in mediations. As such, despite the difference in its scale, the EU's approach should be analysed, scaled down and mirrored in Singapore. A way forward may be to adapt the training programmes carried out by the Bars and Law Societies under the Mediation Development Toolkit, to programmes that may be implemented by existing infrastructures in Singapore such as SIMI and its QAPs. By establishing a national standard, training programmes can be developed to train mediation advocates.

V. Singapore's standards

Despite the progress made in Singapore's context in recent years, mediation is still in its early stages. Having a broad and general set of guidelines that SIMI QAPs can refer to will be an encouraging step. With reference to IMI's Criteria, a set of possible mediation advocacy standards has been proposed in Annex A.

The proposed standards are targeted at training mediation advocates for a facilitative style of mediation. In a facilitative mediation process, the mediator strives to have parties participate in mediation and develop broad interest-based options for resolution.[26] Mediation in Singapore ranges from an "active involvement in the substantive outcome of the dispute using evaluative or directive approaches to a more facilitative model where the focus of the mediation process is to assist parties to achieve a settlement by managing the process of negotiations between them".[27] The Singapore courts have adopted a "facilitative" approach,[28] emphasising parties' concerns and choices with reference to how their dispute should be resolved. This is further illustrated in the State Courts' Code of Ethics on Court Mediation which stipulates that the mediator is to "help" the parties. The values that are emphasised are "respect" and "empowerment".[29] At the SMC, which administers private commercial cases, the established process is "[a] solutions-driven, problem-solving process... [where the] key to mediation is that parties make their own decisions, often with the help of their lawyers".[30] It is clear from the language that SMC promotes and offers a facilitative model.

That said, in the Singapore courts, there are hints of the evaluative model where the mediator plays a more proactive role by "telling" parties what to do.[31] One of the reasons for the use of the evaluative model is the belief in Singapore that people have a cultural preference for an evaluative authority figure acting as a mediator.[32] Where judges are the mediators in court mediation, the "Settlement Judge adopts a proactive stance... by suggesting and actively engaging in the finding of possible solutions to the disputes".[33]

Every case that goes for mediation as part of the court process encompasses three distinct stages: (1) Pre-mediation stage, (2) Mediation and (3) Post-mediation stage. In all stages, the mediation advocates play the same role of being a collaborative problem-solver and this can be broken down into actions that the advocate can take at each stage. As mentioned earlier, a mediation advocate's role is to advise his/her client and to contribute to the mediation in a collaborative and constructive manner. The standards seek to help advocates perform such a role in a facilitative-styled mediation. An example of such a standard could be that mediation advocates should assist their clients in brainstorming for possible solutions that meet both parties' interests.

VI. Conclusion

Mediation advocacy standards would serve to propel Singapore's mediation services internationally and allow mediation to gain a foothold domestically. Needless to say, the implementation of such a scheme will not be easy and will require a few years to take hold. More has to be done to promote the importance of mediation advocacy amongst lawyers to displace the assumption that mediation advocacy skills are a given if they are trained litigators.

Annex A

Mediation Advocacy Standards

(1) Pre-mediation stage
Role: deciding whether mediation is the appropriate dispute resolution process and preparing client for mediation.

Case analysis

- Knowledge of when the dispute is suitable for mediation and the appropriate timing to suggest going for mediation
- Identification of client's interests and distinguishing it from position
- Identification of client's Best Alternative to Negotiated Agreement (BATNA)
- Analysing the other parties' case

Meeting with the client

- Explanation of the mediation process to guide the client on what to expect
- Explanation of the role of the lawyer and the mediator
- Assisting client in adopting an attitude of openness and respect for the other party and the mediator
- Preparing client for his/her strengths and weaknesses in the dispute and brainstorm how to use these constructively
- Analysing information about the other party
- Examine possible points of impasse with client and how to move past them
- Carving out points of negotiation and strategy for the mediation
- Establishing of authority

(2) Mediation
Role: providing emotional and legal support to client

- Supporting and guiding clients by augmenting clients' communication
- Adopting a collaborative approach and being respectful towards other parties

Problem definition stage

- Identification of other parties' interests and positions
- Encouraging client to speak for him/herself as much as possible
- Sharing information to help other parties get a better understanding
- Exploring all issues on the agenda

Problem-solving stage

- Consider other parties' interests in approaching problem-solving
- Assist client in brainstorming for possible solutions that meet both parties' interests

- Reality-testing client and/or other parties if necessary
- Ensuring that settlement agreement covers all agreed items
- Ensure clarity, viability and enforceability of settlement agreement
- Ensure that client has read the settlement agreement prior to signing it

(3) Post-mediation stage
Role: assist clients on future procedural steps

- Rescheduling another mediation if necessary
- Taking opinion from client regarding the mediation

Decoding the B.S. (Behavioural Science) in Mediation

Utsav Rakshit

I. Abstract

Words Matter. Think of how it can be said better.
Else words can cause irreparable damage.
Think of the surrounding context
That wraps your message.
Think of the subtext
And how it
affects
what you
try to communicate
Think of possible biases
How do they influence us?
If you knew more about them,
How would you reframe the frame?

What you say has a mirror effect.
Frame them well. Words Matter.

II. Introduction

I must profess that writing an abstract for a chapter on "framing" requires abstract framing. The words convey the essential message that I hope to convey through this chapter. However, more critically, it is very likely that the first thing that would have caught your eyes is the symmetry in the concrete poetry. I am not going to second guess your interpretation. That said, I am confident that the framed words would have evoked some thoughts or some questions that might have a stronger message than the words itself. Similarly, whether you call a national shutdown a "lock-down" or a "circuit-breaker" effectively means the same thing, yet they have very different connotations.

Being in the business of communication where words are our tools, I believe it is imperative to be more conscious and aware of the impact that our words have and how to best deploy them. With greater awareness of such use, I hope that we get closer to fulfilling the grand promise of mediation.

In this chapter, I will explore the theories of two key cognitive biases that have been explored in the field of psychology and behaviour economics. These are: (a) Endowment Effect and (b) Framing Effect. I will then transplant them into a mediation context and highlight how framing and reframing can be employed to (i) overcome or (ii) capitalise on those biases. This framework is illustrated in Figure 1.

Cognitive bias is a systematic deviation from the rational norm in thinking which influences the choices that people make. While such a pattern varies from person to person, understanding general trends observed in other fields can be beneficial to ensure better outcomes in mediation. In this chapter, I will explore the use of frames to address these biases. Framing can be defined as the process of "constructing and

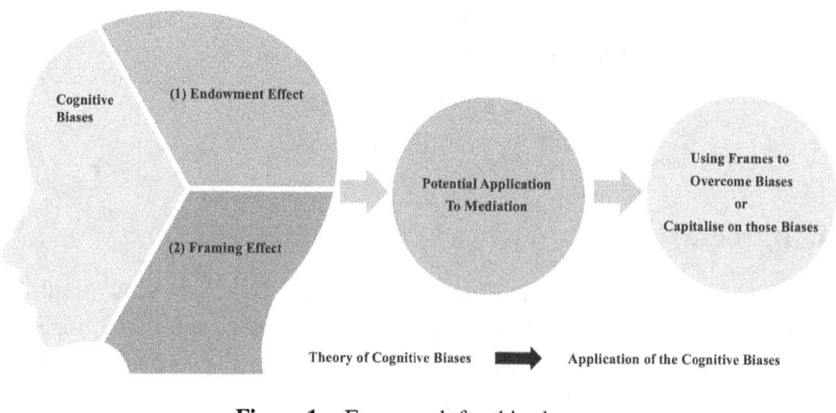

Figure 1. Framework for this chapter

representing interpretations of a situation".[1] The chapter will capture the perspective of both the mediators and the parties in addressing the frames. How can mediators facilitate discussions to go towards productive option generation while making the party evaluate the weakness or strength of their alternatives? Similarly, how can parties invite the other party to consider their options?

III. Endowment Effect

A. *Application in a mediation context*

In a mediation setting, difficulty can arise when there is a significant disparity over what one party is willing to pay and what one party is willing to accept. This would likely happen in the option generation or brainstorming stages. Often in such scenarios, there is a likelihood of an impasse or a breakdown in communication because bridging the two worlds seems like a herculean task for both the parties and the mediator. This section shows how the Endowment Effect can be applied to mediation as a means to overcome a deadlock situation.

B. *Theory of Endowment Effect*

The Endowment Effect is a very well established and explored theory in psychology and behavioural economics. Endowment Effect departs from the rational theory norm. The rational theory operates on the premise that a person is a rational agent and is able to take into account factors like their preference and cost benefit to consistently pursue the best outcome. On the other hand, Endowment Effect is predicated on the belief that people are far more likely to keep an object that they have ownership over than an object which they do not own, even if they are objectively of the same value. An oft cited example is Daniel Kahneman's mug experiment. In that experiment, one group of participants (Group 1) were given free mugs. The other group (Group 2) was not given anything. Group 1 had to quote a price to sell the mug while Group 2 had to quote a price to purchase. The results indicated that there was a wide disparity between the median quoted price for selling the mug (\$7.12) and purchasing it (\$2.87).[2] This experiment illustrates how owners are far more likely to overstate a price for their item than the buyer, as they have a greater sense of ownership over it and are resistant to losing it. A similar point was illustrated by Ziv Carmon and Dan Ariely, where some participants were given tickets to sell, and they quoted a price 14 times higher than what others were willing to pay for them.[3]

(1) *True basis of the theory*

There are three reasons behind the occurrence of the Endowment Effect, namely, loss aversion, psychological inertia and a sense of ownership. These reasons are illustrated in Figure 2 and elaborated in the following. The reason behind one's bias toward their item may vary depending on the item or the context. It is important to highlight these potential underlying reasons as this can provide a basis to identify the appropriate approach to overcoming or capitalising on the Endowment Effect.

(a) Basis 1: Loss aversion?

The proposed underpinning of the theory proffered by Kahneman was loss aversion. This is based on two premises. Firstly, there must be a reference point of the valuation of the good. Secondly, decreases in the objective value of an attribute would bear greater significance on the valuation than a similar increase in objective value.[4] Frames are narratives and

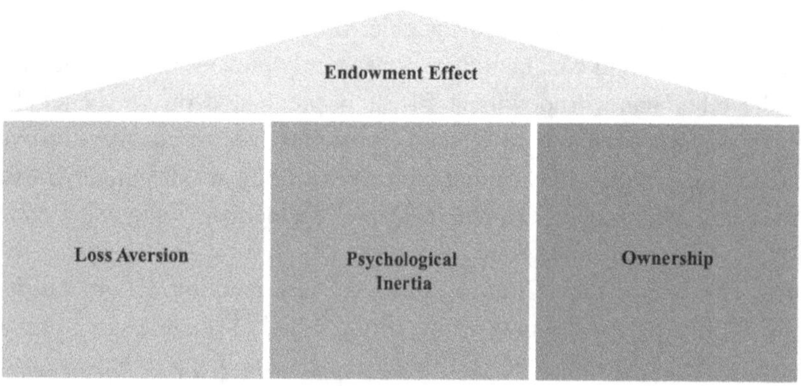

Figure 2. Underlying theory behind the Endowment Effect

angles that can calibrate and influence the reference point. Therefore, by virtue of that, frames have influence over the ultimate choice that is taken.

(b) Basis 2: Psychological inertia?

There are however other contradictory justifications for this theory such as psychological inertia propositioned by David Gal.[5] By drawing parallels to Newton's First Law of Motion, Gal argues that the Endowment Effect is rooted in psychological inertia. This is predicated on two principles. Firstly, motive drives behaviour. Secondly, preferences tend to be fuzzy and ill defined. To explain this, he draws upon an example of a person not wanting to exchange a dollar bill in his pocket for another dollar bill. This phenomenon would not be explainable through the loss aversion reasoning because there was no loss in this case. Instead, this is due to individual preferences being often irrational, as they are unable to objectively valuate their item.

(c) Basis 3: Ownership?

Another basis for the theory is the ownership rationale. The key argument is that a person becomes attached to their possession.[6] When an attachment is established, it becomes a feature of the person's identity, synonymous with the person's conception of himself. As a result, the potential loss then becomes perceived as a self-threat.[7]

(d) Summary of the basis

It appears that all the rationales are equally plausible given that the Endowment Effect can be supported by several justifications. This opens up the effect to multiple applications and the reasoning would ultimately be context specific. In a mediation setting, it would be important to first ascertain what is the underlying reasoning for the disparity. Is it loss aversion, a psychological inertia, or a sense of ownership towards the item? Moreover, it would be useful to deduce whether the "mark-up on the value" is due to an interest of the party itself, or a form of bias that is obstructing the actual interest of the party. An assessment of the underlying interest would indicate the strategy one party or the mediator can use to reframe the offer and move the discussion forward.

C. *Navigating the Endowment Effect in mediation through frames*

As mentioned earlier, the reason behind the occurrence of the Endowment Effect differs in varying contexts, and the approach to addressing this bias depends upon its underlying reasons or motivation. These approaches can be used to overcome the bias, or be capitalised upon to bring forth a productive discussion. The following will show how the underlying reasons behind the Endowment Effect can be applied in the mediation setting.

(1) *Applying different rationales*

(a) Loss aversion

If the underlying cause of the endowment effect is loss aversion, the mediator should focus on reframing the discussion by finding an objective basis to derive the value of the item in question. This could be through some reference to objective standards, thereby addressing the legitimacy issue. When an unbiased mediator, and thus an objective third party, makes some observations about a valuation, there is inherently an element of fairness in their valuation. It also invites the parties to move away from their positions to an uncharted area that might still be within their interest.

(b) Psychological inertia

If the primary reason is a party's psychological inertia, the mediator can reframe the discussion by highlighting the alternatives and exploring the best alternative to a negotiated agreement (BATNA) or worst alternative to a negotiated agreement (WATNA). This would highlight the difficulty of remaining on the path of least resistance. It will also bring to the forefront the potential consequences that would flow from it. Conversely, the mediator could place emphasis on the advantages of coming to an agreement. These include the benefits of cost savings, time savings, moving on from emotional turmoil and other intangible aspects of the deal.[8] Inevitably, these would invite the parties to relook at the offers on the table from a different perspective.

(c) Ownership

If the primary reason is due to a strong sense of ownership, it would reveal that the party has a close affinity and connection with the item. In such a scenario, instead of attempting to overcome the Endowment Effect, it might be better to recognize and work around it. This approach was first noted by Roger Fisher, who suggests to parties to "look for items that are of low cost to you and high benefit to them, and vice versa".[9] Mediators can adopt a similar stance. By reframing the scope of options to a much broader one, more options can be created. With a wider range of options to pick from, the possibility of asking one party to give up something that he has a close affinity with is reduced. Another move that the mediator might make is to speak to the other party to drop the request for the item because that would cost "less" to them than to the person owning it.

(d) Conclusion

There have been major criticisms of the widespread acceptance of the theory in legal scholarship. Klass and Zeiler have famously critiqued the endowment theory by arguing that recent data and leading theories indicate that ownership and loss aversion are no longer the best justification for the disparities in amount offered and the amount that is acceptable.[10] These concerns stem largely from the oversimplified experiments that were conducted and the conclusions that have been extrapolated.[11] Furthermore, as shown in the previous section, there can be more than one justification for such a bias to exist.

If the Endowment Effect is to be applicable in the mediation context, there is still much-needed research to be done to explore what the underpinnings of this bias are, and what approaches should be taken to address each of them, or many of them simultaneously. One way to achieve it is through Fisher's method of digging through to explore the underlying interests of the parties. It may also be the case that other more specific approaches need to be used. Nonetheless, the Endowment Effect is an important concept to alert us to the disparities in valuation that may arise in mediation. By being aware of it, we can then frame and reframe the options accordingly to address bias.

IV. Framing Effect

A. *Application in a mediation context*

Right from the opening statement in a mediation setting, both parties will try to adopt and assert a frame that is in line with their personal experience and perspective. Bodtker and Jameson[12] have likened this to some sort of bidding war to ensure that each party's interests are truly covered. There is also an underplay of controlling the narrative to charter the course of the mediation to obtain a more favourable outcome. This will persist throughout the outlining of issues, the interest gathering stage, option generation stage and till the end of the mediation.

The mediator, on the other hand, would have a different conception of framing. His or her challenge will be to firstly focus on the mutual frame between the parties and expand the overlapping area as depicted in Figure 3. As the mediator starts to find and highlight these overlaps in the

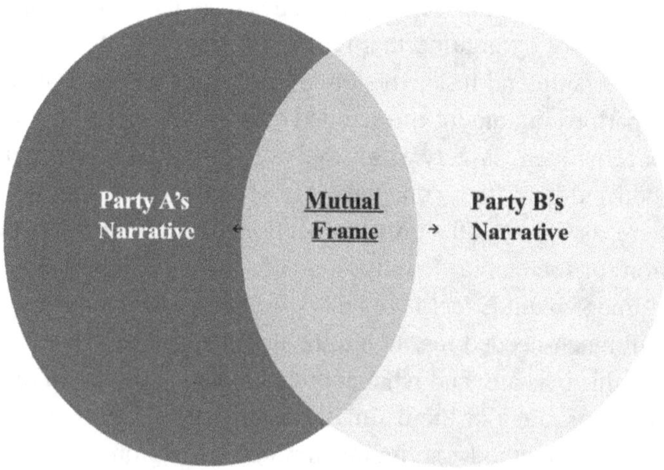

Figure 3. The mediator's mastercard template

narratives, he or she creates common ground for both parties to work from. Secondly, he or she will also facilitate the process of aiding one party to understand the other party's frame. This process occurs throughout the entire session and is particularly useful in a private session, where the mediator has greater latitude to speak openly.

B. *Theory of Framing Effect*

The Framing Effect is best characterised as a form of cognitive bias where people choose options not contingent upon the merit of the option but on how it was presented. Kahneman in his seminal work comes to the conclusion that "logically equivalent statements (evoking) different reactions make it difficult for humans to be rational" when making decisions.[13] In a mediation context, there might arguably be scope for more irrationalities (depending on the nature of mediation). Therefore, people are susceptible to the effect of framing, and not necessarily reality.[14] How something is presented will affect the attractiveness of what they will posit. Levin explores three framing approaches, namely, risky choice framing, attribute framing and goal framing, to provide a useful framework on how certain information can be presented and whether to amplify the positive or negative dimension.[15]

Firstly, risky choice framing is a method used where one highlights the probability of reducing losses, rather than emphasising the probability of acquiring gains. This makes one more susceptible to making riskier decisions. This was demonstrated by the "Asian Disease Problem".[16] The key takeaway from this study was that participants had a higher propensity for taking risks when this was presented as a possibility of reducing losses rather than increasing gains.

Secondly, attribute framing comports with our general understanding of framing where focusing on the presence of positive attributes in an item is more effective to bring about a positive response than focusing on its lack of negative attributes. For example, a beef marketed as 75% lean will be considered "healthier" than a beef marketed as 25% fat.[17]

Finally, goal framing indicates a propensity for people to place more emphasis to act when the negative consequences of not making a particular decision are highlighted, rather than the positive consequences of the decision.[18] This was illustrated through a study which revealed that women were more likely to go for breast self-examination when the information highlighted the negative aspect as opposed to the benefits of going for it.

C. *Navigating the Framing Effect in mediation through frames*

(1) *Different frames*

(a) Risky choice framing

As previously discussed, risky choice framing is where one highlights the reduction of losses rather than the acquiring of gains to persuade. The risky choice framework would be applicable particularly when there has been a loss of trust between the parties, yet there is a need to work together in the future in order to reduce further loss. In such a scenario, a preferable approach would be to focus on the reduction of loss than focus on the possibility of gains. According to this hypothesis, doing so will allow the other party to take a leap of faith and take greater risks in coming to a solution. The risk in this context will be to place trust in the other party, despite their past misgivings. This is corroborated by the formulation of strategic trust as shown in Figure 4:[19]

Therefore, in scenarios where trust has been eroded, an understanding and willingness of mutual loss aversion is likely to enable greater strategic trust. Otherwise, by framing it entirely on what each party stands to gain, it is unlikely there will be as much strategic trust because there might still be questions on the willingness of the party to act in the interest of the

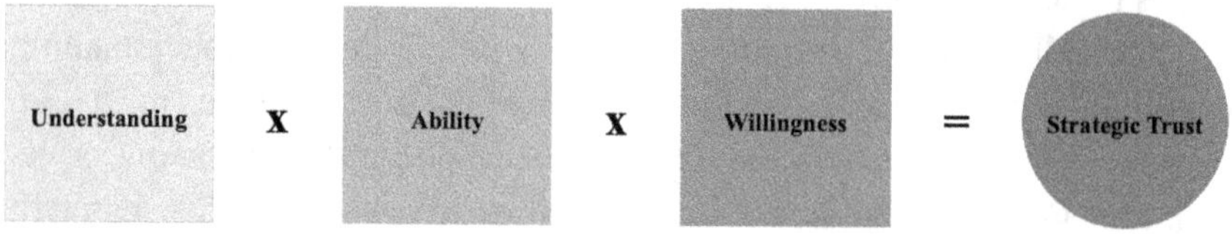

Figure 4. Formula for strategic trust

other party. This is despite the fact that both parties stand to benefit. Hence, if there is an understanding that Party B is likely to suffer loses if there is no commitment to the favoured option, it is more likely that Party A will be more assured that Party B would not renege on their promise since doing so will be tantamount to Party A acting against its own interests. Therefore, there is a strong opportunity to leverage on the common downside that both parties face by framing the issue in such a manner.

(b) Attribute framing

As mentioned, attribute framing[20] has an ubiquitous application in the mediation context, where one focuses on the presence of positive attributes rather than the absence of negative attributes. Much of it is determined by the frame through which the information is conveyed as the default strategy. These would go towards building emotional trust, what Lee describes as a "warm, fuzzy feeling which is neither accurate nor reliable."[19] Parties may often get embroiled in the dispute and may deviate from the ideal framing needed for a constructive and collaborative conversation. This is where the mediator steps in to recharacterise and reframe the message by filtering out the negativity.

Nonetheless, parties that focus on positive framing will likely see an improvement in communication, which will have a ripple effect on addressing options, understanding interests and establishing commitment.

(c) Goal framing

Goal framing highlights the benefits of framing the negative consequences of a decision rather than the positive consequences of making the decision. A negative framing of the consequence is more instrumental in persuading the other party to act on an option. This once again predicates on the loss aversion concept, where the "losses loom larger than the gains".[21] In mediation, mediators can use this to reality test the parties and explore the potential BATNA in order to reconsider the merit of coming to an agreement at the mediation. Similarly, other parties may capitalise on a party's fear of "losing" in order to galvanise support for a settlement.

(d) Conclusion

At first blush, it would seem that positive framing would always be the solution to combat cognitive biases. However, as has been shown by Levin's model, a negative framework can be useful in risky choice framing (where the party wants to invite the other party to take up a risky option) and in goal framing (where negative frames are more persuasive). In general, I would submit that a negative frame is far more effective when it concerns a strategic issue. The fear of losing acts as a glue to encourage the parties to be collaborative.

However, in almost every other aspect of a mediation, a positive frame is imperative to ensure that parties are able to maximise opportunities and build rapport at the mediation. Such aspects involve interest gathering, communication, options, legitimacy and relationship.

V. Conclusion

Endowment Effect and Framing Effect are only two out of the long list of cognitive biases that exist and are applicable in the context of mediation. These include the Ikea Effect, Confirmation Bias, Contrast Effect, Focusing Effect, Barnum Effect, Hostile Attribution Bias, Illusory Correlation and Zero Sum Bias. As posited, it is vital for the mediator and the parties to be sensitive towards the inherent cognitive biases that may potentially be a roadblock to a successful mediation. Understanding the natural human tendencies and psychological motivations instils a greater degree of sensitivity. Framing and reframing steps in to navigate and overcome the challenges that biases pose.

Yet, at the same time, one should also be cautious about the way such biases are used. Mediation is supposed to be a process that is conducted in good faith. In the process of taking advantage of a potential blindspot, one party should refrain from exploiting the other party to their detriment because that goes against the very spirit of mediation. It comes as no surprise that "frame" in a colloquial sense comes with a negative connotation.

In summary, as has been shown, framing and reframing are powerful tools to overcome cognitive biases. But with that power, comes great responsibility.

Banking on Mediation: A Critical Analysis of Financial Disputes Mediation in Singapore

Terence Yeo

"*Just as 'the deceived investor will not invest', complainants with no confidence in a financial dispute resolution scheme will not make use of it...*"[1]

I. Introduction

To have a peerless financial system, there must be an accompanying first-rate dispute resolution system capable of retaining the confidence of consumers.[2] A sound financial disputes resolution (FDR) scheme assures consumers that their rights would be safeguarded, thereby increasing market participation and capitalisation.[3]

This chapter seeks to analyse the state of the FDR scheme in Singapore, focusing specifically on the mediation process. Section II of this chapter sets out the existing structure of the FDR scheme in Singapore. Section III assesses the financial disputes mediation process based on the following criteria: expeditiousness, fairness, transparency, costs and accessibility. It will be seen that while the financial disputes mediation scheme in Singapore is laudable, there is still room for improvement in terms of transparency. Finally, Section IV concludes by outlining possible changes to the scheme such as instituting safeguards to address power imbalances.

II. Financial disputes resolution in Singapore

In Singapore, the FDR scheme is conducted under the auspices of the Financial Industry Disputes Resolution Centre (FIDReC), a public company limited by guarantee.[4] FIDReC was launched in 2005 as a one-stop centre for the resolution of disputes between consumers and financial institutions (FIs). Its jurisdiction extends over all disputes brought by individuals and sole proprietors against FIs, who are members of FIDReC, with exceptions such as disputes over commercial decisions.[5]

Before a dispute is brought to FIDReC, the consumer must first bring the complaint to the FI. Consumers who approach FIDReC without attempting to resolve the dispute with the FI will be referred to the institution.[6] This provides FIs with the opportunity to manage the dispute on their own terms. Once the consumer can show that the FI was unable to resolve the complaint satisfactorily within four weeks of receiving it, the dispute can be brought before FIDReC.[7]

The actual FIDReC process can be separated into three stages. First, at the Case Management stage, the Counselling Service assists the consumer in a preliminary review of the case based on the facts and documents provided,[8] verifying that it falls within FIDReC's jurisdiction.[9] After the preliminary review is completed, the consumer is afforded time to consider whether to lodge a formal complaint against the FI.

Secondly, if the consumer decides to proceed, the dispute would move into the Mediation stage. There is no claim limit for mediation at FIDReC.[10] At this stage, the case manager facilitates dialogue between the consumer and the FI to help them understand each other's concerns.[11] The case manager has no jurisdiction to make any determination or monetary awards,[12] and will only guide the parties to negotiate a mutually acceptable settlement if they are inclined to do so. Mediation may be conducted through telephone or email, but where appropriate, mediation conferences can be fixed to allow for face-to-face communication.[13] Most of the claims at FIDReC are concluded at the Mediation stage. For example, in financial year (FY) 2018/ 2019, about 85% of cases were resolved at this stage.[14]

Finally, if the dispute cannot be resolved by mediation, the consumer can choose to proceed to the Adjudication stage. Adjudicators with relevant expertise will rule in favour of either the consumer or the FI after both parties are given the opportunity to present their case. No external lawyers are allowed to act on behalf of either party at this stage.[15] The maximum award for compensation is S$100,000 per claim. If an award is made in favour of the consumer, it will be binding on the FI but not on the consumer.[16] Where consumers decide against accepting the award, they are entitled to pursue the claim through other avenues such as litigation or arbitration.

Before evaluating the FDR scheme, special mention must be given to the FIDReC Non-Injury Motor Accident Scheme. [17] It is compulsory for all non-injury motor accident (NIMA) claims below S$3,000 to first be mediated and adjudicated by FIDReC before the claimant can commence court proceedings.[18] The Scheme was set up to reduce the judicial resources required to adjudicate low-value NIMA claims and ensure their timeous resolution.[19] When it is clear that the dispute cannot be resolved by mediation, FIDReC will appoint another mediator to indicate whether an award is likely to be made in favour of the consumer and, if so, the likely quantum of the award.[20] While the indication is not binding, it helps the parties understand their position before deciding whether to proceed for adjudication.

III. Evaluation of financial disputes mediation in Singapore

The set of criteria used to evaluate the financial disputes mediation scheme is adopted from the United Nations Guidelines for Consumer Protection (UNGCP). The UNGCP is relevant because it establishes a framework for the implementation of *consumer protection* laws at a national level.[21] It sets out the standards for dispute resolution mechanisms including that of mediation.[22] Specifically, the UNGCP provides that Member States should maintain mechanisms to enable consumers to obtain redress through procedures that are "*expeditious, fair, transparent, inexpensive and accessible*".[23] These criteria also dovetail with FIDReC's core principles of effectiveness, fairness, accountability, independence and accessibility.[24]

A. *Expeditiousness*

Expeditiousness can be defined as the promptness with which disputes are resolved. It is perforce important for financial disputes to be resolved in a timely manner because delays may be emotionally draining on the consumer. This is especially so when the claim involves a significant amount of the consumer's finances. For example, during the financial crisis caused by the collapse of, *inter alia*, Lehman Brothers, many working-class Singaporeans lost extensive savings on their investments and were understandably distressed.[25] The urgency of the situation spurred the Monetary Authority of Singapore (MAS) to work with FIDReC to establish a fast-track dispute resolution process for claims relating to the crisis.[26] Further, the prolonging of the FDR process may divert energy and resources away from other profitable opportunities, resulting in greater losses to the consumer.

In general, financial disputes mediation in Singapore can be considered expeditious. While there is no specific information on the length of FIDReC mediations, the turnaround time for complaints to be resolved by FIDReC is generally short.[27] For instance, in FY 2018/2019, 94.1% of all complaints received were resolved within six months and 99.6% were resolved within nine months.[28] Hence, even considering the efficiency of the Singapore judicial system,[29] mediation under FIDReC is certainly faster than litigation. One possible reason for the expeditiousness of FIDReC mediations is the flexibility of the process (which can be conducted through email, telephone or face-to-face), which engenders great convenience to consumers and representatives from the FIs. Credit should also be given to the nature of mediation, where parties "can craft the solution themselves, allowing them to obtain a speedier and timelier solution that can bring about meaningful change to an unacceptable solution".[30]

B. *Fairness*

Unlike expeditiousness, the criterion of "fairness" eludes simple definition.[31] However, most of the literature recognise that fairness can entail both substantive and procedural elements.[32] Substantive fairness relates to the fairness of the *content of the agreement*, whereas procedural fairness is concerned with the fairness of the *process of reaching the agreement*.[33] Since this chapter seeks to analyse the financial disputes mediation process in Singapore, in the absence of information on the outcomes of FIDReC mediations, it is appropriate to consider only the notion of procedural fairness.

A key measure of procedural fairness is the *mediators' competence to conduct mediations*.[34] In this regard, FIDReC mediators are relatively well-trained because they have to complete the FIDReC Training Programme for Mediators of Financial Disputes (FTPM) before they can be accredited as a mediator.[35] As its name suggests, the FTPM is tailored for the resolution of financial disputes, which necessarily involves specific technical knowledge.[36] Mediators who satisfy more stringent requirements, such as the successful resolution of a minimum number of disputes, will be awarded higher levels of accreditation.[37]

It has been argued that to avoid conflicts of interest, the standards and regulatory body should be distinct from the organisations that administer the training and assessment.[38] Hence, FIDReC's failure to separate standard-setting from the training and assessment of its mediators may invite questions about transparency, quality and accountability. However, FIDReC's one-stop approach can be justified on the basis that the FTPM builds on FIDReC's experience of managing and resolving financial disputes.[39] It is thus arguable that FIDReC is the most qualified organisation to manage and assess its own specialised training. Moreover, there is strong oversight over the FIDReC dispute resolution process. For example, FIDReC is required to submit to MAS a categorised summary report of all disputes received, on a quarterly basis.[40] This system of checks and balances ensures that there is accountability within the FDR process.

But mediators do not only have to be impartial, they should also be *seen to be so*.[41] A commentator has questioned whether FIDReC is fair, given its ties to the financial industry.[42] While the MAS provided the initial start-up funding for FIDReC, it is sustained by the contributions of the FIs.[43] This perception of potential partiality is further entrenched by the monopoly status that FIDReC enjoys as the sole approved FDR scheme.[44] Taken as a whole, it is understandable why concerns arise as to whether there is "a subtle bias at FIDReC in favour of the hand that feeds it".[45] That said, FIDReC tries to maintain some independence through the composition of its Board of Directors, which include individuals without any ties to the financial sector.[46] Concerns on procedural unfairness are also less palpable with regard to the mediation process since it is the parties themselves who will ultimately determine what is a "fair" outcome and not anyone else (including the mediator).[47]

C. *Transparency*

FIDReC drives transparency by disclosing information on the nature of claims it is involved in and the success rates of mediation within its Annual Reports. One may however question FIDReC's practice of not disclosing any information on mediation outcomes. Some commentators have posited that mediation "sweep[s] injustices under the carpet by dealing with each individual dispute privately, so that bad practice attracts no publicity and no precedents are set for the future".[48] By not providing details on the outcomes of mediated settlements, consumers may not be assured that their rights would be adequately protected.

D. *Costs*

Costs would undoubtedly be one of the foremost considerations for consumers choosing between dispute resolution methods. This is even more so when the consumers have already suffered pecuniary losses and are seeking to recover them. In most cases, mediation will present itself as the most cost-efficient option.[49]

Mediation under FIDReC is appealing because it is offered *free-of-charge* to the consumer.[50] Only when the case proceeds to adjudication would the consumer be required to pay a small case fee.[51] The affordability of FIDReC mediation is praiseworthy when it is juxtaposed against comparable FDR schemes around the world. For example, consumers wishing to participate in mediation by the Hong Kong Financial Disputes Resolution Centre (FDRC) are required to pay HK$1,000 for claims valued at less than HK$200,000 and HK$2,000 for claims valued at between HK$200,000 and HK$1,000,000.[52] It must also be emphasised that legal representation is not allowed for FIDReC mediation, which further reduces the costs involved for consumers.[53]

E. *Accessibility*

In a survey of the FDR schemes of the ASEAN 5 countries,[54] the results showed that FIDReC covered the widest ambit of financial services.[55] Prior to the establishment of FIDReC, consumers looking to resolve insurance disputes would have to approach the Insurance Dispute

Resolution Organisation (IDRO) while dissatisfied customers with complaints against banks would have to take the matter to the Consumer Mediation Unit (CMU). The subsequent integration of the dispute resolution schemes for Singapore's financial sector "arguably promotes accessibility by simplifying identification of the relevant ADR entity".[56] Consumers can now turn to a *single* dispute resolution entity that covers a broad range of financial services. Presently, there are over 500 FIs who have subscribed to FIDReC,[57] as mandated by the law.[58]

To enhance accessibility of its services, FIDReC "adopted a strategy which eschewed traditional expensive mass media advertisements".[59] Instead, it formed working partnerships with other mediation and dispute resolution bodies, as well as consumer groups. These include the establishment of referral systems with the Consumers Association of Singapore and Community Mediation Centres.[60] Such partnerships not only ensure effective promotion of FIDReC's services but also help keep its operational costs low.[61] Further, FIDReC works with related campaigns such as the MoneySENSE National Financial Education Programme to raise awareness about its services.[62]

The FIDReC process is continuously finetuned and streamlined to ensure maximum accessibility. Its operational hours are extended until 7.30pm, twice weekly.[63] This ensures that FIDReC's services are available to consumers who are only able to meet up with its officers outside of traditional working hours.[64] Another example would be FIDReC making its Dispute Resolution Form available online for consumers.[65] All in all, FIDReC has done a remarkable job in ensuring the accessibility of its services.

IV. Suggestions for changes

A. *Safeguards to address power imbalances*

It was posited that "[t]he risk of mediation, being an unregulated form of 'informal justice' — enjoying a quasi-regulatory authority without the safeguards that are built into litigation — is that it can mask power imbalances in the relationship between parties".[66] Indeed, as compared to litigation, there is no element of scrutiny by third parties during the mediation process. This concern of unequal bargaining power is especially relevant to FIDReC since its complainants are often not able to comprehend the complex workings of financial instruments. As a result, consumers may not recognise the true value of their claims, which disadvantages them in negotiations with FIs.[67]

It is commendable that FIDReC mediators are not confined to any style of mediation. In a facilitative model, which is interest-based in nature, the role of the mediator is to facilitate communication between the parties generally.[68] The problem is that the "solution is negotiated, but not required to be principled".[69] This essentially circumscribes the role of substantive law since the legal merits of the case is of little relevance to the settlement of a dispute. Thus, there may be concerns of unfairness where the consumers have inadequate negotiation ability. The facilitative model can be distinguished from the *expert advisory* model, where mediators provide the parties with appropriate technical-legal information and benchmarks.[70] They also advise on the merits of the case, suitable settlement terms and likely outcomes should the matter move on to a determinative proceeding such as arbitration or litigation. The drawback of the expert advisory model is that it may diminish party autonomy and neglect the interests of the parties.[71]

However, more focus should be placed on addressing the disparity in the state of knowledge between the FI and the consumer, allowing the latter to make a more informed decision on whether to accept the settlement.[72] The mediators should be made aware of regulatory and legal guidelines and share such information during the mediation process. This would be similar to the Ombudsman process in other jurisdictions. Although both parties cannot be assisted by lawyers formally retained, they should also be encouraged to seek advice from family members or other advisors, whenever possible.

B. *Enhancing transparency*

FIDReC can consider enhancing disclosure of its mediation outcomes. One way to do so would be through the anonymised reporting of dispute details, keeping in mind the need to ensure confidentiality. The value of such information is in fact evinced by the statutory exceptions to disclosure of mediation communication. Under the Mediation Act, mediation communications may be disclosed for research, evaluation or educational purposes if there is no likelihood of revealing the identity of the party involved.[73]

In the case of FIDReC, the disclosure of mediation outcomes would allow consumers to appreciate how common disputes are likely to be resolved. While it is acknowledged that every case turns on its own facts, such "precedents" would assist the parties in making informed settlement decisions.

C. *Expanding the list of eligible complainants*

As mentioned, FIDReC's services are only available to individual consumers or sole proprietors.[74] When MAS first launched a consultation prior to the setting up of FIDReC, there was feedback from respondents that the list of eligible complainants could be expanded to include small businesses using a turnover test to define such entities. However, MAS stated its preference for FIDReC to focus on retail consumers, given that they are "less financially able in comparison with small businesses and more likely to require the services offered by FIDReC".[75] It did however indicate that it was open to reviewing this position in due course.

MAS' position at that time was understandable as FIDReC was an entirely new scheme and there were other teething problems.[76] In its early years, FIDReC was also swamped by the monumental task of resolving the slew of claims involving Credit Linked Notes.[77] However, more than a decade has passed since the launch of FIDReC and the time is ripe to expand FIDReC's jurisdiction. Small and medium-sized enterprises are often branded as part of the "sandwich class" who face concerns about access to justice in civil litigation due to the exorbitant costs.[78] Since FIDReC now possesses the experience and resources, it should make its services available to this particular group of consumers.

V. Conclusion

There are three contributions made through this chapter. First, it has outlined the financial disputes mediation scheme in Singapore. Secondly, it has examined the state of the scheme using the UNGCP criteria. To recapitulate, the system is expeditious, fair, inexpensive and accessible. But more can be done to improve its transparency. Finally, three suggestions for changes were provided. Safeguards were proposed to ameliorate potential power imbalances in the mediation process. The limited disclosure of mediation outcomes and an expansion to FIDReC's jurisdiction were also mooted as recommendations.

As Singapore continues to establish itself as a financial hub, it must constantly review and improve its FDR scheme. It is thus important for MAS and FIDReC to ruminate on the issues discussed in this chapter.

Why Not Have the Best of Both Worlds? A Framework to Interlink Collaborative Law And Mediation to Resolve Personal Disputes

Archa Rajeevi

I. Introduction

Over time, the things that people dispute about have ranged widely. While certain personal disputes can be overlooked, many personal disputes[a] carry a character of intimacy and trust, alongside feelings of refusal or betrayal. On one hand, when such disputes arise or remain unresolved, it can be an emotionally devastating experience for the parties involved.[1] On the other hand, the sourness that arises out of these disputes can remain long after the dispute has been resolved.[2] Today, various methods of dispute resolution promise to be the one-stop shop for settlement of disputes. But if that is really the case, hybrid models such as med-arb would have never come about.

While mediation as a method of dispute resolution has proven to be an effective method to resolve disputes, criticisms range from power imbalances[3] to cognitive biases to neutrality issues.[4] Collaborative Law ("CL") is a relatively a new concept when compared with mediation or arbitration.[5] It has been informally referred to as mediation without the mediator.[6] In this context, this chapter proposes a framework to incorporate

---

[a] See Section III A. for a detailed description on personal disputes.

aspects of CL to an existing mediation framework to resolve disputes that involve personal and intimate relationships.

Very often, new dispute resolution options are created by amalgamating the advantages of two or more discrete dispute resolution processes.[7] Thus, interlinking the strengths of both mediation and CL could provide for a hybrid method that could generate greater opportunities than what would normally exist in mediation for parties to settle their disputes early and not carry forward any bitter feelings after the settlement of the dispute. The chapter looks at developing a hybrid model to strengthen the mediation of personal, intimate disputes and the compatibility of the same. It further looks at how the existing frameworks can contribute to each other and ultimately concludes with the right circumstances in which the hybrid method should be incorporated and the impact of its limitations.

II. Removing blurred lines: what is mediation and collaborative lawyering?

Mediation and CL are similar in many ways. In fact, it might be hard for the disputing parties to notice the differences between these processes.[8] However, beyond blurred lines, there are several differences between both processes.

Mediation is an interest-based process by which an individual helps other individuals and entities resolve differences.[9] Mediators use various methods and models to facilitate dialogue and empathy between the disputing parties.[10] Ultimately, a compromise, agreement or settlement is reached, as the parties begin to gain insight into the other party's perspective and construct new propositions.[11] The mediator serves as a neutral third party who helps the parties come to a resolution between them without making any impositions on them. This is done either with the parties themselves or by involving their lawyers.

Mediation is usually preferred over adjudicatory mechanisms in family or personal disputes[12] because of its informal, non-adversarial, voluntary and confidential nature. It allows the parties to stay in control of the process and ultimately in the outcome of the decision. Since the mediator serves as a guide, helping them along the process by identifying the strengths and weaknesses of the dispute and injecting new perceptions using parties' insights, parties feel empowered as they make their own decisions, as opposed to the decision-making process being out of their control as in adjudication.[13] On the whole, it helps tone down the sensitivity and emotional elements that usually inflame the conflict in personal disputes by using a conciliatory approach and finding a common breakeven point between the parties.[14] It helps parties step out of their positions and identify options to form creative solutions and effective results that are more likely to endure.[15] Very often, mediators may also conduct caucuses and implement a sort of shuttle diplomacy to ensure that they clearly understand parties' interests.[16] Mediation can also work out to be cheaper and quicker than adjudicatory mechanisms depending on the requirement and involvement of the parties.

On the other hand, CL is a relatively newer dispute resolution process. It tries to combine collaborative aspects of mediation and negotiation between the parties without the assistance of a third-party facilitator.[17] In CL, the clients and their lawyers enter into a written contract called the participation agreement to resolve their dispute without resorting to litigation. The contract stipulates a disqualification provision, whereby counsels must withdraw and will be disqualified from representing the parties in litigation if the parties decide to take the matter to court. In such a case, the parties would have to appoint new lawyers.[18] In addition to this, CL also has a discovery process built into it. If required, professionals or experts can be assembled to help the parties resolve their disputes.[19] They could for instance be mental health counselors, financial advisors, child specialists, etc. As the negotiation moves forward, the parties, their lawyers and neutral experts, if any, exchange information among themselves for an efficient settlement of the dispute. On the whole, CL gives the parties involved a real potential to put dispute settlement at the forefront and might allow for a quicker resolution of the dispute when compared to adjudicatory methods.

Both the processes have their own strengths as a means of dispute resolution. CL is similar to mediation in many ways such as being an interest-based, non-adversarial and voluntary process attempting to find the underlying needs of the parties. However, it also has many standalone aspects such as promoting a form of interest-based negotiation through a written contract.[20] Furthermore, while not all mediations require lawyers to accompany the disputing parties, parties in CL must be represented by a counsel. In addition, mediation does not have a discovery process built into it and often does not have the counsels collaborating or exchanging information with each other, without the assistance of a mediator. While mediation can precede or succeed litigation, the CL process starts at the outset and precedes litigation. Finally, there are no mechanisms for caucuses in CL. Parties often remain together in one room with their counsels and professionals, if any to resolve their disputes.[21]

Despite its differences, can the strengths of CL be incorporated into mediation to encourage parties to settle early and more effectively? Is a hybrid method necessary when mediation has been effective?

III. Looking beyond mediation: compatibility of the processes

A. *Do personal disputes need a hybrid model?*

For the purpose of this discussion, a reference to personal disputes would mean disputes between two or more individuals that have an intimate, private character and not those that are commercial in nature. These would include family disputes, matrimonial disputes, disputes between neighbors or even personal injuries that are civil wrongs, for instance. In these kinds of disputes, it is true that when the gun stops firing, the smoke settles.[22] However, frequently, the disputing parties still have to live with each other, at least metaphorically, if not literally. Any damage done during a dispute resolution process can scar future relationships or a potential to have one between the parties. Neither the words nor the actions can be taken back. The bitterness and the cost, both emotional and financial, stay long after.

For instance, in a highly emotional and traumatic family case, the use of a mental health professional as a mediator can turn the mediation session into a therapeutic one and may risk the mediation drifting into topics that are medical in nature.[23] An even better example would be when parties are unrepresented in mediation. There is a possibility of the lack of knowledge and power imbalance producing inequitable results and long-term implications. Therefore, there is a pertinent need to explore and diversify options at hand.

B. *Moving beyond a known recourse*

Mediation is a framework that has proven to be extremely successful in resolving personal disputes since its inception in the 1970s. However, there exists several areas of discontent such as the debate on the neutrality of the mediator, the mediator's approach and values,[24] and the association of mediation's outcome with the contact hours of the client.[25] There also exist critiques such as a party with lesser economic power or women, feeling pressured due to social conditioning to compromise, especially when there is a history of domestic violence or the mediator appears to have gender bias while settling the dispute.[26] Ethical issues concerning mediation have also been raised, such as power imbalance and the mediator's use of power and pressure to settle. In a sense, mediation may, in fact, contain coercive elements.[27] These limitations in no way suggest that the mediation framework is ineffectual. In light of these issues, it is perhaps time to take stock of the situation and explore ways in which the framework could be improved by a hybrid process. A consequential question here would be — could a hybrid process be achieved while preserving the respective strengths and removing the weaknesses of the two dispute resolution options that it seeks to combine?

C. *Why is the combination a perfect fit?*

(1) *Foundation in interest-based consensus and non-adversarial model*

In the CL process, the disputing parties and their lawyers, in signing the participation agreement, explicitly agree to negotiate in good faith.[28] This is done in a cooperative, non-adversarial manner as the lawyers facilitate interest-based negotiations between the parties.[29] In pursuance of its non-adversarial approach, the parties agree to avoid litigation and threat of litigation throughout the negotiation process. Even obtaining interim relief must be done only by consent.[30] Mediation only varies in terms of how it is practiced and the written contract. Otherwise, it is also a non-adversarial approach in which a trained third party elicits positions of the parties and facilitates interest-based discussions between them to bring about a consensual win-win agreement.[31] Therefore, there are more similarities than differences between CL and mediation. It is because of this identical nature that the processes can work together to bring an effective resolution.

(2) *Informality, voluntary consent-based and confidential nature*

In formal adjudicatory mechanisms, judges make the law by enacting formal rules. The process is rigid and parties may potentially have to deal with outcomes they did not expect.[32] Consent and confidentiality may not always exist. In contrast, both mediation and CL cannot begin without the consent of the disputing parties. In essence, the parties have to voluntarily consent to set the proceedings in motion, with the exception of mandatory mediation.[b] Further, parties also have to voluntarily consent to internal aspects within these proceedings such as the extent of disclosure by a mediator in a joint session after a private caucus or to appointing experts or specialists in a CL process. The final outcomes are confidential and are not known to anyone other than the parties involved.[33] These elements are essential in personal disputes due to its intimate nature. In such a case, combining these merits into one hybrid model would be beneficial for resolution of personal disputes.

(3) *The forward-looking aspect*

Both mediation and CL are essentially forward-looking. In essence, mediation focuses to resolve the dispute by eliciting interests and options from positions that the parties hold and CL goes a step forward with the added discovery and exploration process. Both processes will prevail as a quicker and more efficient method of dispute resolution for a foreseeable future. They are flexible and put resolution of disputes at the forefront, which is why they can be effectively combined into one model.

---

[b]For the purpose of this discussion, reference to mediation does not refer to mandatory mediation or any court ordered mediation.

IV. A collaborative framework: collab-med?

The first step for the parties is to appoint their respective counsel. The counsels thereafter collaborate to draft a participation agreement which stipulates the guidelines and conditions for the process to occur, including clauses on the process to appoint the mediator, ground rules for any experts invited and a disqualification clause. Thereafter, the parties and their respective counsel come together for a two-way meeting to collaborate and discuss the basics, issues, concerns and any particulars of the case. At this juncture, free discussion and collaboration is involved. The parties then meet with the mediator and continue to proceed with the normal mediation process.

As a next step, the mediator can use private caucuses and joint sessions to promote dialogue and rapport between the parties. There could also be direct interaction and exchange of information between the parties and their counsel, in addition to the mediator's suggestions, subject to the mediator's ground rules and approval. The mediator and the lawyers can then take stock of the prevailing circumstances and decide whether to call

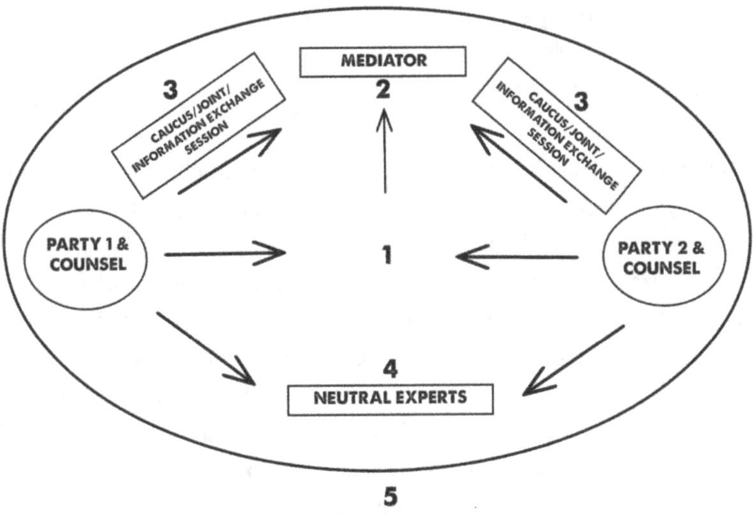

Figure 1. The collaborative framework

experts or specialists, if the seriousness of the dispute requires. In essence, it would involve the parties in a four-way meeting.

On the whole, the process would involve five steps. The framework can be better understood by the illustration shown in Figure 1.

V. The breakeven point: how can advantages become a trump card?

A foremost objective of this framework would be to consider the raft of possible solutions for the dispute. While it is true that the objective of both mediation and CL is to achieve a satisfactory outcome, with this hybrid process, it is not just the mediator but also the respective counsel who help the parties arrive at a resolution. One significant advantage is that the parties contract out of the court process and commit to reach a negotiated solution.[34] Having an agreement binds the parties to stay committed, work cordially in a fair, honest and transparent manner. This also has an impact on the working relationship of the mediators and the counsels as they have to work collaboratively alongside their clients for the common good. The risk of failure (in the context of the disqualification agreement) serves as an incentive for the parties to remain at the table. The initial two-way meetings and the subsequent four-way meetings have the potential of maximising transparency, accountability and possibility of a creative solution. It could also minimise any bias or power imbalance that might occur.[35] On the whole, it makes the process less coercive and more persuasive.

The counsels and clients can make use of an anchor statement at the first two-way meeting. The statement outlines aspirations and sets the tone, laying emphasis on the forward-looking process.[36] This way, the parties will be familiar with the issues to be discussed and facts to be gathered before the mediation process begins. When the mediation begins, the agenda can be set with issues discussed and solutions explored at the client's pace. Further, the option to bring in interdisciplinary expertise to the table, if required, would help untangle the dispute, rather than slice through it.[37] The fact that there are two groupings (the counsels and mediator) to help the parties proceed and resolve the dispute, transforms the process from one of delegated responsibility to one of mutual responsibility. The subtle sense of hierarchy that exists between a mediator and client in mediation or the counsel and client in CL is replaced by one in which the clients take the centre stage and become active rather than passive players.[38] The informal discovery and the agreement combined would prevent information from being withheld and bring added transparency.

Yet another advantage is the suitability of this framework to personal disputes, which often involve high tension and complex emotions. The framework comprises several layers that give parties the required time and space to explore their feelings, and to tone down and feel comfortable with their inflated sentiments. In essence, this hybrid model would provide them a safe and relaxed atmosphere to overcome their issues. The exchange of dialogue, the ability to build rapport and direct interaction give added party autonomy. The counsels also take up responsibility to manage the process and aid their clients to discard arguments and accusations in favour of resolution.[39] Unlike in mediation, the lawyers can give legal advice and draw up legal documents.[40] The model also takes a holistic approach to encourage, discuss feedback and produce final outcomes that are consistent and clear. However, despite the model's workability, it also has its drawbacks.

VI. But can it be a one-stop shop? — the impact of limitations

A primary concern with this model is the cost. Involving a team of professionals to resolve the dispute would mean that parties have to spend more than what they would normally spend, if they chose one of the processes. The increased costs also create an indirect pressure to settle as they would incur far greater expenses if they go to court. In addition, there are also concerns about the nature of the contractual structure underpinning the process. The participation agreement, the confidentiality provisions and ground rules need to be clearly specified and subject to the satisfaction of both parties.

Thirdly, the existence of the disqualification agreement may make the counsels exert undue pressure on the clients to settle, even if the solution is not advantageous to the client.[41] Furthermore, in spite of the disqualification provision, one client can deliberately force termination, for the sole purpose of triggering automatic disqualification. In a way, it can be used as a stalling tactic. Finally, not all cases may require or be suitable to use the proposed model. For instance, if it is a relatively straightforward case that can be effortlessly solved through mediation or a case where the clients are unwilling to be represented by counsels or engage in collaborative discussions with the other party, there is no need to involve a host of professionals and processes. In the end, the suitability and willingness of the parties involved can prove to be an obstacle for the model's applicability.

VII. Conclusion

In mediation, the focal point is on the efforts of one person, the mediator. Neither the parties nor their counsel collaborate with each other. They are predominantly reliant on the skills, perception and persuasiveness of the mediator. In CL, the focus is not on one person, but on the collective ability of all the parties involved.

The hybrid model seeks to combine the processes and shift attention to collaboration itself. It proposes a system whereby the parties, their counsel and the mediator put in effort to find solutions, to listen and build on each other's ideas and suggestions. It is with this integrated effort that the parties can find a third and better way to resolve the dispute. To achieve that, it is essential that everyone in the group relies on each other's insights, creativity and open discussion. The model proposes to combine existing methods to locate shared interests and find a solution that goes beyond compromise in personal disputes.

The ultimate goal is not to create a meeting point for positions and options generated by the parties, but to go beyond it. That is, to find a synergy of ideas that is more than a mere compromise and leads to an effective settlement of disputes and emotions, by satisfying the interests and needs of the parties through a collaborative approach.

The Functions of Artificial Intelligence in Mediation

Chloe Chua Kay Ee

I. Introduction

In February 2019, history was made when a robot mediator settled a three-month dispute in less than an hour in a public court in England.[1] The robot in question, SmartSettle ONE developed by ICan Systems, replaced a human mediator in the dispute concerning £2,000 in unpaid fees claimed by a trainer from a client following a personal counselling course. It did so via a sort of blind-bid mechanism which allowed parties to make offers and counter-offers by moving flags along sliders — a green one seen by the other side, and a yellow flag which is not. By learning the bidding tactics and priorities of the parties, SmartSettle ONE helped to nudge parties into a settlement without revealing their negotiating strategies and secrets. Despite this watershed moment for Artificial Intelligence (AI) in conflict resolution, many are of the view that such technology may only be effective within the confines of small, generally straightforward financial claims. While it is undeniable that there is a great deal of nuance and subtlety involved in persuading people to do things they think they don't want to do, who is to say that AI can never step into the shoes of an experienced negotiator or mediator? This chapter explores the current and future potential of AI through the ways it has helped and can help human facilitators of conflict resolution and ponders upon the age-old sci-fi question of whether the human role is ultimately a dispensable one.

II. Definition

From an optimistic point of view, the potential of AI is seemingly limitless because the very notion of "intelligence" is without limits and likewise without general consensus. Is our current reality that far off from creating the likes of Robin Williams' Bicentennial Man or Star Wars' C-3PO? Hollywood-generated ideals aside, AI is defined essentially as *machines that exhibit capabilities typically associated with human beings*, with a particular emphasis on elements of **autonomy** (i.e. the machine should be able to make decisions without other entities intervening) and **proactivity** (i.e. the machine should take the initiative of changing the state of the world).[2] This cognitive ability that is akin to human initiative and adaptability marks the distinction between "weak" AI and "strong" AI, the latter of which has yet to be achieved according to philosopher John R. Searle.[3] Searle is known for his 1980 Chinese room thought experiment which argues that a digital computer executing a program cannot be said to have a consciousness of its own no matter how intelligently or human-like the program may make the computer behave because ultimately whatever it is producing is meaningless to the computer. This goes a step beyond the test proposed by Alan Turing in 1950 where, if an objective third party cannot tell the difference between letters written by a person and a computer, then the computer is considered intelligent.[4] As the very concept of intelligence is fluid to begin with, it is no wonder that the philosophical tests for what constitute AI, and the quality of AI, have evolved with time and technological advancements. The relevant question here is to what extent can a mere simulation of a human mind, with no intentionality and conscious understanding of what it is doing, help to improve conflict resolution processes.

III. Functions of Existing AI

A. *To organise*

As it turns out, "weak" AI already has its fair share of contributions to dispute resolution. At the most basic level, there are tools available to analyse huge amounts of data and documentation. Brainspace is an electronic discovery software used to detect and sort unique phrases in large data sets, allowing humans to examine a pool of 2.7 million documents in under two hours. To further enhance organisation, the Clustering algorithm is a method that attaches its own labels to groups of documents and clusters together documents with similar themes.[5] While these tools greatly convenience their human users and save time and manpower costs, they are rudimentary devices meant at best to play a small supplementary role. The reality today is that this form of AI is the most readily accessible norm with a slow adoption of more advanced AI. However, the negligible levels of autonomy and proactivity — which correspond to limited competence — displayed by these programs discourage widespread acceptance of furthering the development of AI to become significantly useful tools in future.

B. *To inform*

On a more advanced level, existing AI also have the ability to inform in a manner which increases consequential awareness for the human user. In 2015, Daniel J. Olsher published an article on a new AI tool called cogSolv.[6] While its primary function is to facilitate first responders on peacekeeping and humanitarian missions in foreign cultures, there is a high possibility of adapting its use for daily dispute resolution processes. cogSolv is able to process complex human situations while retaining their nuance, using flexible, brain-inspired algorithms processing. This enables the program to generate remarkably human-like inferences across complex social systems. It makes social factors such as religion, culture, values and history much easier for outsiders to understand and take into account. For instance, when giving an illustration of how Western governments could go about handling anti-LGBT sentiment in Africa, the article shows what cogSolv would generate as "recommended" (invoking religious or community concepts) or "disfavoured" persuasion elements (secularism, colonialism, human rights discourse).[7] Essentially, the tool indicates exactly what to emphasise and what (and how) to avoid in order to maximise persuasive effectiveness from parties' points of view. One can imagine how helpful a tool like cogSolv could be for cross-border mediators, particularly when faced with matters like the Hague Convention where parties come from different cultures which are foreign to the mediator. It would allow the mediator to better understand which issues are more fixed to a party and thus less amenable to negotiation and areas where there may be more room to consider the other parties' perspectives.

Another feature of cogSolv is its "sentiment engine" which, using deep semantics, identifies the emotional impact behind parties' words. Although the example given was for opinion mining of tweets/social media content, this could be adapted for daily alternative dispute resolution (ADR) to better ascertain the meaning of parties' words (especially when there is a cultural or contextual difference that hinders understanding) or to uncover what is intentionally being hidden (for situations like domestic abuse). However, while Olsher extols the many virtues of cogSolv, it is a rather recent invention and not much else has been written about it. One cannot help but wonder if it is almost too good to be true.

C. *To predict*

An extension of the ability to inform is the ability to predict. A key problem-solving methodology employed in many existing AI projects is Case-Based Reasoning (CBR) which relies on the key assumption that if a new problem is similar to an old one, it will have a similar outcome.[8] In the legal domain, CBR can provide interpretation shortcuts, warn for potential errors or suggest lines of thought.[9] For mediation advocates, this information can also be handy when it comes to reality-testing and reminding certain parties why ADR is preferred over litigation. For instance, the AI project Split Up makes predictions about the distribution of marital property following divorce in Australia.[10] Mediators too could use these predictions to their advantage either by using it as a guideline for themselves, or using it to remind parties what is at stake or still worth fighting for, depending on the context.

Many programs were developed based on CBR rather than a Rules-Based System (RBS). RBS is a set of procedures guided by rules which follow instructions of the type *IF condition THEN conclusion(s)*.[11] While RBS is essentially a set of procedures guided by rules, CBR aims at capturing and using knowledge from past experiences which allows known solutions to be applied to solve similar problems. There is thus a greater guarantee of the prediction's alignment with reality and the task of problem-solving is improved.

One of the earliest programs, the MEDIATOR,[12] attempts CBR almost all the time while it is in operation. While attempting to achieve reasoning goals which come up during problem-solving, the MEDIATOR first attempts to use case-based inference to achieve the goal. If no case is available, or if the available case(s) cannot provide a solution consistent with the rest of the problem specification or solution, the MEDIATOR uses an appropriate "from-scratch" method. The MEDIATOR's memory is generally able to provide at least one case to use each time it is asked for a case.

D. *To recalibrate*

Despite being one of the earliest case-based problem-solvers in need of a lot of fine-tuning and work, the MEDIATOR's greatest beauty is in its constant ability to treat every failure as feedback and incorporate it into the system. When a proposed solution fails, the MEDIATOR treats it as feedback and attempts to understand why the solution was bad and whether it could have avoided it. From this, the MEDIATOR then tries to come up with a better solution. The program treats blame assignment and failure recovery as problem-solving tasks.[13]

Given that human mediators are only human at the end of the day, they might not have this robotic capacity to reframe their thoughts and deal with their emotions in as efficient a manner as AI programs are capable of.

E. *To replace*

Ever since the MEDIATOR, many other programs have been created with the main objective of the AI acting as mediator or negotiator, controlling the process and its flow. More often than not, these programs are based on CBR.

Notably, the computer program PERSUADER[14] uses CBR to learn from its experience (much like the MEDIATOR) and it is also based on decision theoretic techniques (multi-attribute utility theory) to provide enhanced conflict resolution and negotiation support in group problem solving. The PERSUADER operates in the domain of labour management disputes and its main task is to act as a mediator, facilitating the disputants' problem-solving so that an amicable settlement can be achieved. Given that labour disputes often involve numerous parties, Sycara notes how AI use is beneficial for group decision-making processes. Sycara finds that computer support could help maintain rationality in decision-making by avoiding emotional clouding of issues; help allay privacy concerns, since participants may wish to disclose only parts of their reasoning and utilities depending on the trust they share with others; enforce fairness in decision-making by precluding domination of discussion by a single party; speed up the decision-making process by enabling rapid generation of proposed agreements of joint benefits to the parties; and provide the means for recognition and resolution of differences in goals and viewpoints.

Perhaps one of the most commercially successful and widely relevant online dispute resolution company today, SmartSettle aims to find the middle ground among parties to settle disputes based on satisfaction functions acknowledged by them. The blind bidding mechanism alluded to in the introduction of this chapter is part of their system. At first, the parties declare their tenure to each item in dispute. The assigned preferences are, however, not static as they may change during the negotiation process, resembling the adjustment of the first choices made by parties. Besides assigning their preferences, parties must decide on what would be a constructive outcome for each one and try to merge it on a single text. During the negotiation process, parties may simply exchange messages or they can rely on SmartSettle to produce suggestions according to the current state of the case, which the parties may or may not accept. When the parties reach an impasse, they may ask SmartSettle for an equal distribution of the items in dispute. It is important in this phase that the preferences are well defined since the allocation of items depends on that. A final document is then produced. This entire process is supported by a website on which the parties log in, access their personal data and perform all the actions related with the negotiation process. SmartSettle appears to be readily accessible and available for the masses. Perhaps, with its historic moment as the first robot mediator to solve a court dispute, it will gain greater recognition and acceptance.[15]

While PERSUADER is used in labour management, the Family Winner is used in the Australian family law domain. The system uses game theory and heuristics with an adapted algorithm. Similar to SmartSettle, parties must input their intended value to each item under dispute in the system. According to these values the system tries to assign the items to the parties, having in mind that each allocated matter may change the preferences of the parties on the other issues. Once this is done, the parties are asked whether they agree with the distribution; if the answer is no, the system embarks on a negotiation item-by-item, starting with the item considered less controversial. This process of decomposition and division goes on until there are no more items under dispute.

Even though these AI systems are available and seem to perform the role of mediator satisfactorily, they are often too niche — belonging to a particular domain of people — or too costly to effectively use in the long-run. As most of them are based off CBR, this is logistically difficult in common law jurisdictions as all cases decided have to go into the program's databases on a constant basis.

More often than not, these systems are designed to handle division of property or monetary claims. These AI programs deal with straightforward situations and rely on a Zone of Possible Agreement. While they could be effective in resolving simple disputes, it is hard to imagine how they would hold up when situations that call for human empathy or understanding arise.

IV. Functions of Potential Future AI

A. *To supersede*

When we imagine AI, we often picture robots or avatars that physically look like humans.[16] They would typically act and sound like humans too. Given that Sophia the humanoid AI robot has been around for a few years now, it is not too far-fetched to imagine an AI that could be our very twin. If we were to program this robot in such a way that it had all the best parts of existing conflict resolution AI (the ability to remember every case that has ever been decided, how every significant mediation reached a settlement, the knowledge and sensitivity of every culture, a constant high level of energy and attention and observation, the ability to turn every failure into feedback with zero emotional encumbrance, the ability to appear neutral to all parties at all times, etc), and program it to mimic human expressions (e.g. dilation of pupils to show empathy, adjusting sitting posture to show a relaxed stance) we could very well create an AI that would supersede our human role in conflict resolution.

It is not an automatic guarantee that human beings are the most effective communicators. We are only human after all and there is understandably a great deal of fallibility. Research has shown that AI can be used to achieve fairly sophisticated interactions with children suffering from developmental disorders such as autism. These social robots have been able to elicit desirable behaviour from autistic children that are not typically demonstrated in their daily lives. These children have also relied on robots to facilitate interaction with third parties.[17] One can imagine that when humans encounter parties that they cannot get through to, AI could well act as a back-up, free of judgement, hesitation and frustration.

B. *To play God*

Ambient Intelligence (AmI) is an emerging discipline that refers to electronic environments that are sensitive to humans. AmI systems have popped up in fields like Networked Home Environments but not yet in the legal domain. Carneiro *et al.*[18] paint a hypothetical scenario where a party attending an online mediation enters an AmI environment. The system is able to monitor the party's behaviour to search for signs of fatigue or stress by analysing the way he moves the computer mouse, the way he types on the keyboard, the way he blinks, etc. The system can sense if his emotions are escalating and try to calm him down by playing his favourite music, cooling the temperature if he is nervous and sweating, advising him to go to the lounge for a break when it senses he is too tense and needs to relax. Crucially, AmI constantly provides the mediator with a representation of the parties' states so that they may make the right decisions given the constraints of online mediation (lack of body language and other non-verbal cues). Such an AmI system does not seem like a faraway daydream, although there are practical considerations involved. Ultimately, it could go a long way in helping parties be more receptive in the conflict resolution process.

V. Conclusion

Artificial Intelligence can be an infinitely helpful tool in conflict resolution with many roles for it to play. The future of AI is immensely exciting and every day we are drawn closer and closer to newer technological advancements. While it has to be acknowledged that AI as it currently stands cannot replace an experienced and skilled human facilitator of dispute resolution, there is no doubt that there is a very real possibility that it one day could.

While Searle might find that AI would never be able to gain the sort of understanding and consciousness possessed by human beings, thus forever rendering it "weak", linguist Noam Chomsky believes that human beings are born with an internal hard-wired set of instructions to learn language, rendering us not unlike AI machines who are pre-programmed with a basic set of instructions for their functions. If human beings could evolve from our basic rules of language to the multilingual communicators we are today, what is to stop AI from developing a Searle-described consciousness eventually?

Confidentiality in the Singapore Mediation Scene: Is It Sufficient or Can More Be Done?

Dinesh Kumar Sukumar

I. Introduction

Confidentiality refers to the obligation of all parties to the mediation not to disclose communications to any third parties.[1] Confidentiality is regarded as one of the cornerstones of mediation with mediators often giving parties unqualified assurances as to the confidentiality of proceedings.[2] Hence, confidentiality conferred on mediation communications might seem unqualified. In Singapore the preferred practice of managing confidentiality during mediation is the in-confidence approach which operates by treating all information disclosed privately as confidential unless otherwise indicated by the disclosing party. This can be contrasted with the practice of open communication where information is not treated as confidential unless specifically requested by the relevant parties.[3] Despite Singapore adopting the seemingly more restrictive of the two practices, mediation confidentiality is in fact not absolute in Singapore.[4]

Confidentiality problems commonly arise where one of the parties to mediation attempts to refer to what transpired in mediation for use in settings outside mediation; or where a third party, including a court or tribunal, seeks disclosure through the mediator or a party or by attempting to access mediation documents; or where a mediator wishes to disclose on a voluntary basis.[5]

This chapter will be assessing the importance of confidentiality in mediation before evaluating, in light of confidentiality's importance, whether the safeguards to protect confidentiality in Singapore is adequate or if it can be improved. From the analysis, it will become apparent that confidentiality plays a pivotal role in mediation and though Singapore is headed in the right direction by increasing safeguards on confidentiality, there is still room for improvement.

II. Importance of confidentiality in mediation

The 2018 Model Law on International Commercial Mediation[6] provides for two levels of confidentiality in the mediation process as reflected in Article 9, "Disclosure of information", and Article 10, "Confidentiality". Article 9 states that no matter raised in private sessions by individual parties should be disclosed to the other party by the mediator. Article 10 is written in relation to the mediation process as a whole and states that apart from the mediator and parties, no third party should be privy to the proceedings. In the former, it is claimed that confidentiality induces candour and provides a safe environment for each party to reveal and reflect on their fundamental concerns.[7] In the latter, it is meant to prevent publicity for mediation proceedings and to avoid adverse consequences for parties in respect of disclosures they might have made.[8] Without confidentiality, parties might be fearful of a landslide of additional lawsuits or other types of bad precedents as what parties said formerly during the mediation can be brought up.[9]

The need to provide a safe environment for mediation, through confidentiality, extends beyond private sessions to joint sessions as both parties are encouraged to engage in a full and frank discussion of their differences with a view to finding a resolution to the conflict.[10] Hence, the efficiency and effectiveness of mediation is increased as mediators are more likely able to identify parties' real positions and interests. This can be juxtaposed against other dispute resolution methods. In litigation, parties are often unwilling to disclose information unless compelled by the court and in arbitration it is common for arbitral awards to be scrutinised by the courts. Confidentiality also protects the mediators' reputation and reinforces their impartiality by excluding them from the pressure of making disclosures during or after mediation.[11] This is important because mediators, unlike adjudicators, have no decision-making powers as they function primarily as facilitators. Thus, they are unable to compel the production of information. Hence, confidentiality enables mediators to gain the parties' trust to encourage forthright communication.[12]

III. Scope of confidentiality

Having established the importance of confidentiality, the scope of confidentiality will need to be determined. This is done by examining the law in relation to the common law, equity and statutory regulations.[13]

A. *Confidentiality in equity*

In equity, persons who receive information in circumstances of confidence cannot make unauthorised use of the information. A court may grant relief if there has been an actual or threatened abuse of such confidential information[14] and where there is no remedy in contract. The High Court in *X Pte Ltd and another v CDE* ("*CDE*") held that the following elements will need to be present before there is a breach of confidential information: (1) the information to be protected must have the necessary quality of confidence about it; (2) that information must have been imparted in circumstances importing an obligation of confidence; and (3) there must be an unauthorised use of the information to the detriment of the party who originally communicated it.[15] While Singapore courts have not considered confidentiality in equity in the context of mediation context, it is submitted that the need for there to be detriment to the party under the third element of *CDE* undermines confidentiality as it places an additional obstacle, which may not always be present, in the preservation of confidentiality. *CDE* was considered in the context of litigation where, unlike mediation, confidentiality is not a key tenet. Hence, as the law now stands, it is unlikely that equity will be applicable to confidentiality in mediation.

B. *Confidentiality in common law*

The common law recognises three types of confidentiality: (1) legal professional privilege; (2) contractual confidentiality; and (3) without prejudice privilege.[16]

(1) *Legal professional privilege*

Communications brought into existence for the primary purpose of existing or contemplated legal proceedings are protected by legal professional privilege and are exempt from disclosure in the event of litigation.[17] Given that the privilege concerns the lawyer-client relationship, it would not be very relevant in mediation where the mediator is supposed to be a neutral third party to the dispute, rather than an advocate for his client.[18]

(2) *Contractual confidentiality*

In practice, most agreements to mediate contain a confidentiality clause which binds parties and the mediator not to disclose any information or documents used in the mediation to third parties outside the mediation.[19] Parties may also be required to sign release forms which state that they will not subpoena a mediator or records of the negotiations for a later court case.[20] However, in order to enforce a contractual claim, where there has been a breach of a confidentiality obligation, the matter would need to be litigated in court. Litigation traditionally favours disclosure and transparency.[21] Moreover, cases are often heard in open court and judgements are public. Thus, the obligation of mediation confidentiality would be undermined.

(3) *Without prejudice privilege*

Communications between parties made on a without prejudice basis during negotiations towards a settlement of a dispute are generally privileged and inadmissible in subsequent court proceedings relating to the same subject matter.[22] Admissibility refers to situations when mediation communications may be properly admitted in court.[23] Therefore, it can be reasoned that confidentiality is a precondition to inadmissibility. Without prejudice privilege is meant to encourage litigants to settle their differences out of court without fear of suffering adverse consequences in litigation if no settlement is reached.

(a) Section 23 Evidence Act

In Singapore, the position of the without prejudice privilege is supplemented by Section 23 of the Evidence Act ("EA").[24] Under Section 23, two different situations are contemplated: (1) upon an express condition that evidence of admissions is not to be given and (2) under "circumstances from which the court can infer that parties agreed together that evidence of it should not be given". While Section 23 restricts the application of the rule only to parties involved in the negotiations themselves, the Singapore Court of Appeal in *Mariwu Industrial v Dextra Asia* ("*Mariwu*") acknowledged that the common law has extended the rule to third parties not being allowed to adduce without prejudice communications.[25] However, the post-*Mariwu* decision, *Ng Chee Weng v Lim Jit Ming Bryan*, seems to have reverted to the narrow interpretation of the rule. The Singapore High Court held that the without prejudice rule applied to communications made between the parties with the assistance of a mediator.[26] Moreover, Section 23 applies only to admissions and not mediation communications in general. Hence, the scope of applicability of the without privilege rule is not altogether clear in common law.

(b) Exceptions to the without prejudice privilege

This uncertainty is compounded by the numerous occasions in which, despite the existence of without prejudice communications, the rule does not prevent the admission into evidence of what parties might have said or wrote. In *Unilever Plc v The Procter & Gamble Co* ("*Unilever*"), the English Court of Appeal listed eight exceptions to the inadmissibility of without prejudice communications.[27] Though the exceptions in *Unilever* have been acknowledged by the Singapore courts, only the first one — using without prejudice communications to determine whether a compromise agreement has been concluded and the terms of such an agreement — has been dealt with by the Singapore courts.[28] Evidence of compromise agreements may need to be disclosed in court for the enforcement of such agreements. While the exception has been held to be "firmly established in the [Singapore] context",[29] the lack of decisive rulings by Singapore courts about the status of the other seven *Unilever* exceptions contributes to the ambivalence of the scope of protection of the privilege.[30]

While not expressly articulated in *Unilever*, the exceptions to the without prejudice privilege are most likely a result of balancing the competing interests in mediation. On one hand, there is an interest in promoting and encouraging settlement of disputes outside the court system and in protecting emerging dispute resolution processes such as mediation which encourage candid negotiations. On the other hand, there is an interest in disputing parties obtaining full discovery, and in courts and tribunals having the best access to evidence and information.[31] For example, parties may want to challenge the fairness of the mediation process, such as a breach of the mediator's ethical duties or the coercion of parties into reaching a settlement.[32] Absolute confidentiality, without judicial oversight, may also harm the interests of third parties while providing a safe haven for participants' wrongdoing or injustice.[33] Hence, it is important for mediation confidentiality to be balanced with the need to maintain integrity and fairness in mediation. To achieve this balance there needs to be a clear articulation of the limits and exceptions to mediation confidentiality. In light of the common law's inability to provide such clarity, the 2017 Mediation Act[34] ("MA") is a welcome piece of legislation which helps to fill the gaps in Singapore.

C. *Confidentiality under statutory regulations*

(1) *Overview of Singapore's Mediation Act*

In the second reading of the Mediation Bill, Senior Minister of State for Law Indranee Rajah clarified that, except under narrow circumstances set out in the act, communications made in a mediation cannot be disclosed to third parties to the mediation and cannot be admitted in court or arbitral proceedings as evidence.[35] The MA sets out the parameters for disclosure and admissibility of mediation communication.[36] It largely clarified existing law at the time of enactment, rather than changing it and so case law preceding the MA may offer guidance in relation to how the MA's provisions may be interpreted by the Singapore courts.[37] This is especially useful since the MA is still relatively new and hence, there is a dearth in case law.

Mediation communications are "protected in two broad ways" under the act.[38] Firstly, mediation communications cannot be disclosed to any third party to the mediation, unless it falls under one of the ten exceptions listed in Section 9(2) such as where all parties to the mediation consent. Hence, a prima facie restriction on disclosure of communications to third parties is created. Short of the exceptions, any further disclosure will require the leave of court or an arbitral tribunal, if the disclosure is being made in the context of arbitral proceedings, under Section 9(3) read with Section 11.[39] The requirement to seek leave prevents vexatious breaches of mediation confidentiality.[40] The MA puts to rest the conflicting positions at common law as to whether third parties are allowed to adduce without prejudice communications. Additionally, mediation communication is defined broadly in Section 2(1) to include "anything said or done" for the purposes of or in the course of mediation and is not restricted to admissions as in Section 23 of the EA.

Secondly, pursuant to Section 10 of the MA, "[a] mediation communication is not to be admitted in evidence in any court, arbitral or disciplinary proceedings except with the leave of a court or an arbitral tribunal under Section 11". The need for leave reflects how the MA has stopped short of creating a statutory privilege that is congruent with the without prejudice privilege at common law. This underscores the importance of public interest in determining admissibility, which is consistent with the common law approach of balancing interests in encouraging settlement against other public interests such as having the best access to evidence in court proceedings.[41] Thus, Section 11(2) lists factors, including "public interest", which a court must take into account in deciding whether or not to grant leave for a mediation communication to be admitted as evidence. However, the phraseology used to describe the court's discretion in Section 11(2), such as the taking into account of "interests of the administration of justice" and "any other circumstances or matters that the court...considers relevant" is vague and does not offer any substantial guidance as to what the limits of disclosure should be. Hence, while the requirement for leave guarantees an additional layer of protection it is submitted that the court's wide discretion is troubling.[42]

(2) *Shortcomings of the Mediation Act and changes which can be made*

Although the MA fills gaps in mediation confidentiality, there are shortcomings. Firstly, the MA's pronouncements on confidentiality and inadmissibility do not apply to all mediation regimes. Under Sections 6(2)(a) and (b) mediation sessions conducted by court or taking place under the court's direction and any mediation proceedings conducted under "any written law" are excluded. The exclusion of certain types of mediation is meant to avoid potential inconsistency with existing mediation frameworks that have their own established rules.[43] For example, Section 19(3) of the Community Mediation Centres (CMC) Act[44] states that evidence of anything said or admission made in a CMC mediation session is not admissible in any proceedings and Section 19(5) lists the exceptions to the general prohibition against admissibility.

However, having different regimes governing confidentiality would be unfair to parties since the amount of protection accorded to their communications is determined by the arbitrary factor of the regime under which their mediation proceedings fall under.[45] At times, parties do not even have a choice as to the mediation regime because the type of mediation is mandated by the court. Under Section 15 of the CMC Act, for instance, magistrates have the power to refer Magistrate Complaints to the CMCs for mandatory mediation. Significantly, there is no reasonable justification for the different treatment of disputes that may result in equally severe consequences.[46]

Secondly, the MA missed the opportunity to create a robust mediation privilege such as in the American Uniform Mediation Act (UMA).[47] A statutory protection articulated as a privilege for mediation communications would have been the strongest safeguard for mediation while affording sufficient flexibility by allowing automatic exceptions where the privilege has been waived and allowing courts to balance the relevant competing interests.[48] Such protection would have put the privilege on equal footing with other established privileges such as legal professional privilege and litigation privilege.[49] It is submitted that this is preferable to the MA's current framework where, though there is a general prohibition against disclosure, there are numerous exceptions which include very broad ones such as "any other purpose that the court or arbitral tribunal... considers justifiable in the circumstances of the case" in Section 9(3)(d). Such broad exceptions are vague and can encapsulate almost all considerations. Hence, the need for the other exceptions in the MA is undermined.

The imposition of blanket rules either permitting parties to raise exceptions without restriction or prohibiting them from ever raising them, "create incentives that are inconsistent with the goals of mediation".[50] Instead a balancing test is a more nuanced way for the court to factor in other considerations alongside the "invasiveness of the threat to mediation confidentiality."[51] Section 6(b) of the UMA provides a useful illustration of how the balancing test could be adopted by the MA, where the consideration is whether the "need for the evidence... substantially outweighs the interest in protecting confidentiality".

While it has been confirmed that the usual civil remedies for a breach of confidentiality, such as injunctions and damages, will be available if unauthorised disclosure is made or threatened,[52] compliance with non-disclosure would be greater if the consequences for a breach were to be translated to actual provisions in the MA.

Finally, the inclusion of practical measures in the MA to preserve confidentiality such as *in camera* hearings for the determination of the admissibility of mediation communications and anonymising the names of parties in the court's grounds of decision would be useful in preserving confidentiality whenever there is a need for the court to scrutinise confidential mediation communications.

The practice of upholding anonymity has been adopted in English decisions such as *AB v CD Limited* ("*AB*").[53] In *AB*, the judge directed that the judgement deciding whether a binding agreement was reached be appropriately anonymised due to the without prejudice nature of the communications and the need for confidentiality about the terms of settlement. Conversely, the Singapore Court of Appeal in *Surindar Singh s/o Jaswant Singh v Sita Jaswant Kaur* ("*Surindar*")[54], when deciding whether an alleged mediation settlement agreement was binding, scrutinised the parties' correspondence post-mediation and reproduced paragraphs which recounted mediation communications.[55] Though it is arguable that the parties might have waived their privilege in *Surindar*, the court's approach appears to be focused on fact-finding and seems to reflect a general lack of sensitivity to the importance of preserving mediation confidentiality.[56] While the court in *Surindar* might have adopted a more conservative approach in its reproduction of mediation communications if it were decided today in light of the MA, there are no provisions in the MA on redacting mediation communications. Hence, it is likely that the same approach would have been adopted. As such, it would be good to have a provision that covers the publicity of mediation communications. In this way, the court is able to access mediation communications, when required, while confidentiality is preserved.

IV. Conclusion

The MA has provided much clarity with regard to confidentiality in mediation communications by shedding light on the principles in the common law which were previously unclear in several regards. The need to obtain leave from the court or arbitral tribunal prior to the disclosure of mediation communications to a third party in Section 9(3) is reflective of the symbiotic relationship between the different modes of dispute resolution. It also highlights how mediation is still at a stage where the court's assistance is required. However, this might change with the Singapore Convention on Mediation ("Convention"), ratified in 2020, which would facilitate the recognition of mediated settlement agreements without enforcement by the courts. As a result of the Convention, there would be less need for court scrutiny of mediation communications. Even then, there are modifications which can be made to the MA. This includes having (1) express MA provisions on the consequences of breach, (2) a balancing test for courts to weigh the protection of confidentiality against other considerations instead of having a list of broad exceptions, (3) practical measures the court can adopt in preserving confidentiality and lastly, if possible, (4) unifying all the different mediation regimes within the MA. The unification of the various mediation regimes would ensure there is greater consistency as a single framework for confidentiality in mediation communications can be achieved. The adoption of these changes in the MA would further strengthen the safeguards to protect confidentiality in mediation.

*Online Mediation: The Future that Arrived Much Sooner Than We Thought**

Mah Hao Ran, Ian

I. Introduction

Online alternative dispute resolution ("OADR") has grown considerably since the dawn of the internet. We can observe this growth from how commentators have described OADR over the years. In the early 2000s, OADR was described as "essentially a change in venue rather than in approach … [and] does not differ very much from the offline process, except for the fact that another form of communication … is used".[1] Some 10 years later, it is recognised that OADR has "adapted and grown into its own separate field" and has "moved beyond trying to mimic familiar, offline processes".[2] Automated processes and online filing systems are but some examples of such new processes.[3]

Despite its rapid growth and how technology has been famously referred to as the "fourth party" in a dispute,[4] OADR has not been fully embraced by most.[5] Academic literature in this area is also not as extensive compared to other aspects of alternative dispute resolution. This is perfectly understandable given that OADR has always been regarded as inferior to face-to-face dispute resolution. As such, the focus has primarily been on analysing the advantages and disadvantages of OADR, and identifying situations where it would be suitable to turn to

---

*The article is written in the author's personal capacity, and the opinions expressed in the article are entirely the author's own views.

OADR.[6] To the best of the author's knowledge, there have not been any serious suggestions that OADR should entirely replace face-to-face dispute resolution, at least not in the immediate future. Recent writings have predicted that OADR will only dramatically change the role of lawyers "[i]n the next decade".[7]

But the future has arrived much sooner than we thought. The global pandemic situation threw the lives of many into disarray. There has been a sea of change in the way we work and communicate due to the imposition of mandatory work-from-home regulations and other lockdown measures. Many industries have been forced to adapt to the evolving situation and the legal industry is not spared. Over the course of the past year, we have seen hearings being moved to online video conferencing platforms, as well as lawyers being called to the Bar via the same.[8] Parties seeking to resolve their disputes may now therefore have no choice but to turn to OADR given the difficulty, or even impossibility, of face-to-face dispute resolution.[9] In this regard, we are, in many ways, propelled into a future that we may not be ready for.

The secondary has now become the primary, and this merits serious consideration as to how we may better utilise OADR in the present, rather than viewing it as a mere future possibility. Specifically, the focus would be on online mediation. Since effective communication, emotional connection and management, and the preservation of relationships are the cornerstones of mediation,[10] mediation would be most affected by a move to online platforms. It is therefore a contemporary issue worth examining. To this end, this chapter first briefly examines existing literature on the advantages and disadvantages of online mediation. Following which, it seeks to draw from academic literature in various disciplines such as language studies, psychology, behavioural sciences and information technology. Practical suggestions on how to assemble a future-ready toolkit for mediators, lawyers, and aggrieved parties alike will be put forward. It is hoped that this chapter would provide some insights as to online mediation and spark interest in its development.

II. All about online mediation

Before delving into the advantages and disadvantages of online mediation, it is important to first be familiar with what exactly online mediation entails. At the risk of oversimplification, there are three main forms of online mediation, each with their own advantages and disadvantages. The first and most common is mediation conducted over the telephone or via e-mails.[11] The second and less common is mediation conducted over video conference.[12] The third is what has been described as a "completely automated online dispute resolution system with no interaction from a third party at all".[13] Examples include "blind-bidding mediation" where parties can choose the settlement agreement via an automated process.[14] This form of online mediation is least common since it is limited to situations where only the settlement sum is in dispute, which is often not the case. As such, it is usually a precursor to the previous two forms of online mediation. Additionally, these are also complementary tools such as online filing and case management systems.[15]

It is also important to understand the situations in which online mediation would be suitable, and Ebner helpfully sets out a list of questions that can aid aggrieved parties in deciding whether to turn to online mediation.[16] This includes, among other things, whether there are geographical barriers, unwillingness to meet face-to-face and scheduling difficulties.[17] All of these factors stem from the advantages of online mediation, which we now turn to.

The most apparent advantage of online mediation is convenience. Due to the online nature, cross-border mediations are made possible.[18] And at least for mediation utilising non-instantaneous forms of communication such as e-mails, parties need not even be available at the same time, allowing for easier scheduling.[19] Such non-instantaneous forms of communications also have the added advantage of allowing parties the space to calibrate their responses more carefully without allowing their emotions to taint their responses in the heat of the moment.[20] This is similar to what Ury famously referred to as "going to the balcony" by taking a step back to regain mental balance and control.[21]

However, the boon of online mediation's decreased interactivity is ironically also its bane. Commentators observed that online mediation suffers from a lack of "media richness", which is defined as the "capacity of the medium to transmit visual and verbal cues".[22] Since e-mails transmit neither visual nor verbal cues, it is the most deficient in this regard.[23] Telephone calls, on the other hand, lack visual cues. An important implication of this is the possibility of decreased levels of trust, because the lack of such cues "develops voids in communication [and] [t]hese voids are filled quickly by psychological doubts and fears".[24] While the reduction in media richness is less severe for video conferencing, certain important cues, such as body language and physical closeness of the parties are inevitably lost in transmission especially if the entire body is not shown.[25]

Regardless of the advantages of online mediation, "there is almost universal agreement that mediation is most effective if the parties to the dispute are physically present before the mediator".[26] This much is not disputed. And this is why we see most existing literature only going so far as presenting the advantages and disadvantages of the various forms of online mediation and pointing out certain situations in which they may be more suitable. The underlying premise is the universally agreed fact that face-to-face mediation is superior and therefore the default. But in light of the current landscape where face-to-face mediation may be impossible, this fundamental premise is no longer absolute. There is thus a need to seriously consider how to neutralise the deficiencies and capitalise on the strengths of online mediation as we can no longer afford to treat online mediation as a mere secondary option or a future possibility; the current landscape has become a turning point where online mediation becomes the mainstay. This changing landscape will serve as a testbed for innovation, experimentation and development of online mediation. Even as we later return to face-to-face mediation, this would result in a more robust secondary form of mediation that we can turn to, which can only be beneficial to all. The next section examines how we can fully realise the true potential of online mediation and avoid pitfalls.

III. Assembling a future-ready toolkit for online mediation

A. *Media richness redefined: A new currency in the age of online communication*

Trust lies at the very foundation of every successful mediation. Without it, there cannot be effective communication and collaboration towards a productive outcome.[27] Unlike other forms of dispute resolution, there is no authoritative neutral third party to dictate the outcome. There must therefore not only be trust between parties *inter se*, but also trust in the mediator's ability to guide the process in the best interests of the parties.[28] Much ink has been spilt over how the development of trust is affected by a move to online platforms, although there is no consensus in this area. While some hold the view that it is much more difficult or slower for trust formation, others conclude that there is no fundamental difference.[29] Regardless, it is agreed, at the minimum, that trust formation is not impossible.

Even if trust formation online is possible, it does not mean the online mediation process will be smooth sailing. As mentioned earlier, important visual and verbal cues are inevitably lost in online mediation due to a lack of "media richness"; nothing is as "rich" as face-to-face communication. This may lead to misunderstandings, especially when there is a pronounced disparity between the sender's perception of the meaning behind a message and the recipient's perception of that same message. Most existing academic literature acknowledge the lack of "media richness" and in turn propose ways to minimise the loss of existing cues and prevent misunderstandings. For instance, some have explained the importance of eye contact and appropriate user-webcam proximity,[30] or even technical details like the optimal frame rate to employ.[31] Some have even suggested the maintenance of "spatial faithfulness" through the use of multi-directional cameras,[32] although such elaborate setups are admittedly not practical in most situations. Further, a quick search online would yield many results on how to improve effective communication over video-conference.[33] Ways to minimise communication mishaps have therefore been fairly explored and parties should consider all of these to improve their online mediation sessions. Yet, we need to go further than this. Can we not only minimise the shortcomings of online mediation but also maximise its strengths and achieve what might be impossible in face-to-face mediation? Perhaps we have simply been measuring the "richness" of online medium against the wrong currency.

The way we communicate has drastically changed with the advent of online communication. This has led to some researchers concluding that many people no longer consider the richness of a medium to be measured plainly by its ability to convey a message unequivocally.[34] A good example to illustrate this would be to look at the language used in online communications. Often times, persons communicating online do not adhere to formal linguistic rules but instead employ spelling innovations and modifications, or copious amounts of abbreviations and acronyms.[35] Therefore, while this may represent an incomplete transmission of a message under traditional media richness theory, that is far from the truth. The rapid development of online communications has perhaps reached a stage where traditional theories can no longer fully explain it. In light of this, it is suggested that there are at least two key aspects parties should be sensitive to in order to fully realise the potential of online mediation and communicate effectively.

First, it is important for parties to be aware of the nuances of online communication. For instance, as regards text-based online communications, the use of the period may be perceived negatively by some, even though it represents proper use of the English language.[36] Yet another feature unique to text-based online communications is the use of emojis, which are images commonly used to convey messages. Research has shown that emojis aid the conveyance of a wide range of emotions and messages, including complex and nuanced ideas like sarcasm.[37] For video-conference, the display picture that parties have on their accounts, for instance, also convey certain messages or mood.[38] These are all features unique to online communications.

Secondly, the way different generations communicate online should also be accounted for. While the younger generation may be adept at or used to employing emojis and spelling innovations, the older generation may adhere more strictly to formal language rules,[39] which may be perceived negatively in the online context.

Language is a constantly evolving creature, but as Grice famously explains, there are certain universal maxims to adhere to for effective communication.[40] For instance, one should avoid obscurity of expression and ambiguity.[41] Imagine the following scenario: A and B are parties to an online mediation and there is a wide generational gap between the two. A uses certain emojis to convey something jokingly, but B does not understand it the same way and interprets A's message literally. A also uses certain phrases that have a completely different meaning to someone of a different generation. Consequently, B misinterprets A's message and the parties fail to reach an agreement. The communication breakdown could have been prevented if both parties had been sensitive to the nuances of online communication and the way different generations communicate online. Admittedly, this might be difficult to always expect of the aggrieved parties or their lawyers. But there is a third party in the mediation — the mediator.

Given the development of international standards and accreditation of mediators, as well as continued efforts to professionalise the industry,[42] it would not be too much to expect mediators to be sensitive to developments and nuances in online communication. This is no different from other competencies that are currently expected of mediators. While the mediator is not expected to be an all-knowing expert of internet language and its nuances, especially since online communication is constantly evolving at a breakneck pace, mediators should at least be sensitive to the hotspots for online communication breakdown. This would include being able to identify signs of such breakdowns early, taking into account potential generational gaps and the resultant differences in the ways that parties communicate. From this, they can then advise parties on potential misunderstandings, explain the meaning of certain phrases and seek out clarifications whenever necessary to prevent communication breakdowns like the one in the hypothetical situation. In due time, they can even advise parties on the effective usage of unique features of online communication, such as emojis, to convey complex messages. These competencies have understandably not been given much attention due to the secondary nature of online mediation, but the current landscape offers the opportunity and incentive to seriously research into this area.

B. *Confidentiality concerns*

Confidentiality is another key aspect of mediation which may be affected by a move to online platforms. Without it, parties may be afraid to speak freely and openly,[43] which would inevitably adversely affect the collaborative process in reaching an outcome. There is also the fear that information disclosed may be used against the aggrieved parties. Confidentiality is therefore of great value to parties involved. However, it may not be as straightforward to ensure confidentiality online.

Unlike face-to-face mediation where notes can be destroyed in the physical presence of all parties, the same cannot be guaranteed online as data may be easily copied or retained long after the mediation has transpired.[44] Notwithstanding this, current legal means of ensuring confidentiality, such as the inadmissibility of statements made on a "without prejudice" basis or an action for breach of confidence,[45] would still apply regardless of the medium. This is therefore not much of a concern.

What is of greater concern, however, is that the use of technology has also exposed the mediation process to multiple risks of leakage of confidential information at each step of the process due to viruses or external contractor error.[46] As such, all relevant parties must have the necessary tools to deal with such concerns. In choosing the appropriate platform to conduct their mediation, parties should always ensure that the security features conform to contemporary industry standards, such as end-to-end encryption. As we have seen over the course of the past year, there have been multiple security concerns over video conferencing platforms such as Zoom.[47] However, we have also witnessed the speed at which such security concerns were addressed and how competitors have eagerly reacted.[48] This is a trial by fire for online communication platform providers. With important meetings and events being shifted online, security standards would inevitably be raised to keep pace and will continue to come under heavy scrutiny. As such, parties must be aware of current security concerns and how to minimise them, as well as exercise prudence in their choice of online communication platform. Just as with how communication has been transformed in the digital age, the improvement of online security is something that has developed independently of mediation. All relevant parties must be keenly aware of such developments and readily draw from them. Only then can the true potential of online mediation be realised.

IV. Conclusion

Online mediation has been both explored and unexplored at the same time. It has been thoroughly explored insofar as it being an alternative to face-to-face mediation or a future possibility. The research so far is primarily focused on when it would be suitable to turn to online mediation.

Due to the current global pandemic, we are forced into uncharted territory where online mediation is no longer just a future possibility but a necessity. In light of such changes, the way we view online mediation and the competencies of mediators must certainly evolve to keep pace. It is hoped that this chapter has offered a different perspective on the role of online mediation.

Nevertheless, it is impossible to touch upon all areas and there is yet more to be discussed. This leaves much of online mediation unexplored. For instance, the way in which online mediation should be taught to better prepare for the current and future mediation landscape is also worth examining.

Exploring What Mediation Looks Like in the Religious Spheres of Islam and Christianity

Sabrina Chau Shu Ning

I. Introduction

Our values and beliefs, including our religious beliefs, inevitably shape the way we view the world and the people around us. It is therefore no surprise that one's religious views would affect the way conflict resolution is carried out. Mediation as a form of conflict resolution exists in both Christian and Islamic communities. However, a mediation that takes place in a religious sphere tends to have a different focus that is shaped by that particular religion. Thus, this chapter seeks to explore how religious mediations in Christianity and Islam deviate from the conventional secular model of mediation. This will be done by comparing the mediation model used by Christian and Islamic communities, with what is done in the secular model of mediation. However, it should be noted that because one's interpretation of the religion, as well as their conformity to that religion is subjective, the ideas discussed in this chapter will be broad generalizations and may not always hold true in every situation.

II. Conventional secular mediation

Before looking at how religious beliefs can change the process of mediation, it is important to first set out what mediation looks like without the influence of religion. Typically, save for the presence of pre-mediation, a mediation is comprised of several stages. Mediation begins with an opening, then goes into problem-defining and problem-solving. When defining the problem, the mediator will generally ask questions to understand the interests of the parties. Then, during the problem-solving stage, he or she will encourage the parties to brainstorm possible options to resolve the conflict. The mediation is successful if the parties are agreeable to a solution.

The role played by the mediator is dependent on the model of mediation followed. Leonard L. Riskin distinguishes the facilitative model from the evaluative model.[1] Riskin posited that a facilitative mediator assumes that his or her principal mission is to clarify and enhance communication between intelligent parties who are capable of creating better solutions than any mediator might create. On the other hand, the evaluative model assumes that the parties want and need the mediator to provide some guidance as to the appropriate grounds for settlement.[2] An evaluative mediator would thus generally go into and advise on the substantive issues of the dispute.

Meanwhile, the facilitative mediator generally refrains from giving advice on the substantive content of the dispute and instead focuses on the process and managing the relationship between parties.[3] The role of the facilitative mediator would therefore be to remain objective and facilitate communication among the parties, thereby pushing the parties to understand their interests and participate in creative problem-solving.[4] It promotes an outcome-focused mentality, aiming to create a win-win result for both parties. This method relies on the self-determination of the parties and assumes that the parties will actually be able to understand the underlying interests at stake in order to come up with creative options and solutions for the dispute.

At the same time, the facilitative model of mediation calls for parties to take an active role in the mediation. Ideally, parties would need to approach the mediation with a collaborative mindset, balancing being assertive and cooperative.[5] According to the Thomas-Kilmann model, a collaborating individual will look out for his own interests and well as the interests of the other party, allowing for the creation of a "win-win" situation. Collaborating involves working together to find a solution that fully satisfies the concerns of both parties. This is unlike other modes of responding to conflict such as "competing" where the individual pursues his or her own concerns at the expense of the other party, or "accommodating", where the individual neglects his or her own concerns to satisfy the concerns of the other party.

Overall, beyond the mechanics of the mediation process, the distinctive aspects of secular mediation come from the roles of the people involved in the mediation. The Singapore model calls for mediators to simply be facilitators, with parties ideally being collaborative in return. For the sake of completeness, it should also be noted that mediation advocates may also play a key part in mediation. However, their role will not be discussed in this chapter.

III. Mediation in Christianity

Christianity shows a clear antipathy to litigation, especially between Christians. In the New Testament of the Bible, the apostle Paul rebukes the church in Corinth saying "To have lawsuits at all with one another is already a defeat for you."[6] Though the Bible seems to give the church authority to arbitrate over matters,[7] the modern church has a clear preference for mediation, with many seminaries offering courses on resolving conflict through mediation.

To a certain extent, the modern church takes direction from the secular model of mediation, using similar skills and techniques. The form of Christian mediation follows the secular model, with the broad stages of mediation remaining the same. However, Christian values add another dimension to the mediation with different biblical principles having a bearing on how the mediation is carried out. Broadly speaking, there are three main biblical ideas that shape Christian mediation. The first and most significant idea is the Christian doctrine of unity within the church. This not only redefines the way conflict itself is viewed, but also affects the way parties will behave in a mediation. On the other hand, the other two Christian teachings mainly impact the mindsets and perceptions of the parties to the mediation.

A. *Unity in the Church*

Turning to first look at the doctrine of unity, it is submitted that the church's emphasis on unity shapes the way conflict is viewed, which inevitably affects how mediation is carried out. Unity among Christians is a biblical principle that is deeply embedded in Christian communities, but is often overlooked in mainstream media. This notion of unity among Christians comes from Jesus Christ's prayer in John, where he prays that "those who believe... may all be one".[8] This emphasis on unity has caused some theologians to see conflict and resentment as the "bait of Satan",[9] suggesting that Satan uses conflict to thwart God's plan of Christians being united. This brings a spiritual element into the idea of conflict and conflict resolution, where conflict is almost viewed as "wrong" because it furthers the scheme of the devil. This affects mediation because, on a macro level, mediation turns into a weapon that can be used against Satan. On a more micro level, the orientation of mediation is changed, which has strong consequences. Instead of conflict being viewed as one party against another, it becomes both parties against Satan. Both parties' interests are therefore aligned, uniting both parties in a common cause against the "bait of Satan". This strengthens the parties' commitment to settle. It also fosters camaraderie between the parties and encourages them to be more collaborative instead of competitive. Therefore, because there is an added push towards being collaborative, the notion of unity within the church enhances the effectiveness of facilitative mediation.

B. *Humility and selflessness*

The second biblical principle, which relates to a certain mentality that Christians should possess, is one of humility and selflessness. The Bible instructs against "selfish ambition and vain conceit", asking Christians instead to humbly value others over themselves, "not looking to [their] own interests but... to the interests of the others".[10] This idea comes from the need to be like Jesus Christ, who is said to have pursued the interests of God rather than his own. If this biblical instruction is followed, it would affect the subjective mindsets of parties. Rather than adamantly insisting on their own interests, this biblical principle pushes parties to reprioritise their interests and consider the wants of the other party. To a certain extent, this spirit of humility and selflessness might prompt parties to be more creative and flexible with their options, being more prepared to meet the interests of the other party. However, if there is a power imbalance, this idea of selflessness might further entrench this imbalance, with the "weaker" party becoming even more willing to give up their interests. For example, if a party were to feel guilty and undeserving, this notion of selflessness might trigger them to simply comply with any demands made by the other party. In a sense, this Christian value encourages parties to be more accommodating rather than collaborative, which deviates from the secular model of mediation.

C. *Love and forgiveness*

The third relevant principle in the Bible is the conviction to love and forgive the people around you, which naturally places more weight on the relationship between parties in a mediation. In Christian theology, the command to love your neighbor as yourself is known to be the second most important law.[11] On the part of the party, this prescribes a certain obligation to love others, and places emphasis on the importance of relationships. If there is conflict between individuals, the Bible coaches them to bear with one another, stating that they should "[forgive] each other as the Lord has forgiven [them]".[12] The need to love and forgive someone shifts the focus of the party from the problem to the relationship, with the goal of the mediation therefore moving to reconciliation and forgiveness. While this serves to motivate the parties to address their past hurts and reach an amicable solution, it also runs the risk of a party overaccommodating to account for these values of love and forgiveness. The effect of this on mediation seems similar to that of humility and selflessness, but is rooted in how the Bible teaches Christians to treat one another, rather than how Christians should view themselves.

D. *Summary*

Overall, while Christian mediation borrows its structure from secular mediation, because its focus is reconciliation and unity, rather than workable solutions, its substance is radically different from the secular model of mediation in Singapore. In other words, while the process of mediation is similar, the purpose of mediation and the roles of people involved depart from the secular model. Even though the emphasis on unity among Christians spurs parties to be more collaborative, this is undermined by the values of humility, selflessness, love and forgiveness, which prompt parties to be more accommodating. These values stress the need to give in to the needs of others and place more emphasis on maintaining the relationship rather than coming up with a creative solution. As a result, mediators tend to focus more on facilitating forgiveness rather than good option generation.

That said, it bears noting that the effect of religion on the subjective behaviour and mindset of the parties is dependent on how strongly the individual subscribes to those beliefs. Values like humility, love and forgiveness do not naturally come to someone who is in a conflict with another. Therefore, Christian mediators would generally need to constantly remind the parties of these values during the mediation. In fact, Christian mediators might have the additional obligation to spiritually guide the parties to follow biblical principles. This unavoidably causes the mediators to be more interventional and evaluative.

IV. Mediation in Islam

Mediation is not unfamiliar to Islamic Law. Islamic teaching places a great deal of weight on peace, which drive Muslims toward mediation. There is a long history of amicable settlement (*sulh*) and arbitration (*takhim*) in Islam, with *sulh* being presented as a legitimate and desirable form of settlement. In fact, the Prophet Muhammad was involved in mediation-like activities within and outside of the Muslim community.[13] It should be noted that though arbitration (*takhim*) is mentioned in the Quran multiple times, it was not conceived of as a distinct form of conflict resolution, but was instead intended to work together with other processes like mediation.[14] This is important because the sentiments from this Qur'anic formulation of conflict resolution bleeds into modern day mediation.

Much like Christianity, the Islamic model of mediation has been influenced by the secular concept of mediation. Islamic mediators are usually trained and experienced in the secular process.[15] However, the Islamic ethos of conflict resolution shapes the configuration of the mediation as well as the psyche of the parties. The Quran states that "[i]f you fear a breach between a man and his wife, appoint an arbiter from his people and another from hers. If they wish to be reconciled God will bring them together again. God is all-knowing and wise."[16] This statement is reflective of two values. The first is the inclination to seek and follow direction issued by a third party, while the second is the belief that reconciliation will be brought about by Allah.

A. *Seeking and following advice of third party*

Looking at the Muslim tendency to seek the opinion of a wise and objective third party, it is apparent that Islamic mediation takes on elements of arbitration. The role of a mediator usually falls on an Imam or an elder whose standing demands respect from the parties. The concepts of *suhl* or *wassatah* are commonly associated with a process of mediation that is conducted by a third party who allocates responsibility and pressures parties to accept the suggested solutions.[17] This approach is understandable, given the Qur'anic command to obey "those in authority above them".[18] However, this affects the role of the mediator as well as the role of the parties.

First of all, the role of the mediator is affected because Islamic tradition essentially enables the mediator to act as a quasi-arbiter. Mediators are asked to "make peace between [parties] with justice… because Allah loves those who are fair and just".[19] This form of mediation leans towards the evaluative model of mediation, where the mediator makes judgement calls and deals with the substantive issues of the mediation. However, it should be noted that this method is distinguished from arbitration in that the outcome of a mediation is not binding and still requires parties to consent to it. Nonetheless, it is clear that fairness and justice are core conditions for an Islamic mediator, with the Quran warning against departing from justice.[20] This differs from secular facilitative mediation where the interests of parties are central and justice is more of a peripheral concern.

Secondly, the role of parties is also affected by this practice of seeking and following the advice of a third party. When directions are given to the mediator, the role of the parties is to follow those directions with "full

[and] willing submission".[21] This radically departs from the secular model of mediation because it prompts parties to be more accommodating. Yet unlike in the Christian context, Muslim parties are made to be accommodative towards the mediator rather than the opposing party. This does not give much space to individual rights and personal grievances because Islam prioritises peace and harmony over the interests of individuals.

B. *Allah causing conciliation*

The other theme that comes from the above verse[22] is the power of Allah to cause conciliation between the parties because he has "full knowledge and is acquainted with all things". This does not just suggest that it is difficult for man to reach a point where there is reconciliation, but also suggests that Allah is in control of all relationships. In fact, another verse in the Quran says to "fear Allah and adjust all matters of difference among you".[23] This has implications on the role of the mediator in a session. Because the relationship between parties is a matter that is settled by Allah, the mediator might have the tendency to ignore the personal sentiments of parties and focus more on simply settling the issue in dispute. In a sense, there is a sort of deference to God with regards to the relational matters. This deviates from the secular model in that the mediator no longer focuses on the communication between parties, but rather looks at what the mediator thinks is "just" in the circumstance. This inevitably causes the mediation to be more prescriptive and less facilitative, not fully taking into account the emotional needs of parties.

C. *Strict adherence to Islamic Law*

The need to adhere strictly to Islamic law also affects mediation. The outcome of Islamic mediation is limited by some of its laws that may void or vary mediated agreements. This inadvertently affects the problem-defining and problem-solving stage of the mediation. Concerning this, there are two points that mediators need to bear in mind. The first is that only problems that concern lawful (*halal*) and wholesome (*tahir*) matters can be mediated over and agreed upon.[24] This essentially means that the subject matter of the mediation cannot come into conflict with Muslim laws and norms because agreements concerning it will be unenforceable. Secondly, one should note the consequences of the Muslim concept of *riba*. Islamic law prohibits usury (*riba*), which is closely linked to the Islamic ban on gambling (*gharar*). This prohibition has been extended by analogy to ban contractual "uncertainty". This means that the law will void any commercial transaction where the party's consideration is uncertain because it might result in one party receiving something of greater value than of what they gave in exchange.[25] Altogether, this means that during Islamic mediations, the parties will need to first ensure that the subject matter of the problem is something lawful and wholesome, and then when brainstorming options, the mediator would need to ensure the solutions adhere to Islamic law.

D. *Summary*

Overall, much like Christian mediations, Islamic mediations do not really change the general process of mediation. Instead, Islamic beliefs shape the underlying tenor of mediation. For example, the legalistic mentality of Muslims creates limitations to the problem-defining and problem-solving stage of the mediation. The role of the mediator and the parties also largely deviate from that of the secular model. Instead of the mediator facilitating and encouraging communication between the parties, the Islamic mediator seems to focus on the subject matter rather than the relationship, and is almost essentially given the authority to judge and decide the outcome of the mediation. On the part of the parties, they are compelled to follow the opinion of the mediator in the spirit of peace and obedience. Therefore, it seems that Islamic mediation greatly departs from the secular model of mediation. In fact, it almost mimics arbitration, with the difference being that mediation requires both parties to consent to its outcome.

V. Conclusion

In conclusion, it is clear that the influence of Christian and Muslim values significantly impacts the entire process of mediation. These differences in values change the entire objective of mediation. While secular mediation is focused on finding good solutions that are in line with the interests of parties, religious mediations have different goals. For Christianity, mediation seeks to restore unity in the church, appealing to Christians to humble themselves and forgive those that have wronged them. While in the Islamic tradition, mediation is conducted in order to maintain peace and pushes Muslims to obey fair directions given by the mediator. However, these are mere generalisations that are subject to the individual subjective nature of humans. Though these general inclinations of each religion help us to better understand the interplay between religion and mediation, this is only the tip of the iceberg. A further exploration might wish to ask how mediators can effectively leverage on the religious beliefs of parties.

Is Mediation an Appropriate Forum for Dispute Resolution in the Context of Domestic Violence?

Tomoyuki Lewis Ban

I. Introduction

Mediation is growing more and more popular around the world in all areas of the law. In Australia, mediation for all practices are available, where most mediations deal with family, small businesses or consumer disputes.[1] Similarly, throughout Asia there has been a significant growth in the importance of mediation. Most recently in 2019, the formal signing ceremony for the United Nations Convention on International Settlement Agreements Resulting from Mediation took place in Singapore.[2] In particular, mediation has been popular in the context of family law, because many feel that the approach of collaborative decision-making is effective and appropriate amidst interfamilial disputes.[3] Nevertheless, there has been much contention surrounding the appropriateness of family mediation when one party has been a victim or survivor of domestic violence. The crux of this contention revolves around the power imbalance between the parties, and the detrimental impact this might have on the equitability of a mediated settlement or resolution. Furthermore, there are also public policy concerns about the ineffectiveness of mediation in requiring the abusive party to take responsibility for the acts of violence or abuse. This chapter will largely focus on exploring the impact of power imbalances in a mediation within the domestic violence context, and thereby evaluate the measures aimed to balance these concerns. Following this, several policy concerns in this area will be discussed. Finally, the last section of this chapter will assess the appropriateness of mediation as a forum for dispute resolution in the context of domestic violence and seek to provide suggestions moving forward.

II. Power imbalance

Power is a fluid term — it can have both positive and negative connotations depending on the context of its use. In the context of mediation, some have defined it as "the ability of a person to influence or modify an outcome".[4] On the basis of this definition, we can describe "power imbalance" as an unequal distribution of these abilities to influence or modify an outcome. In this regard, advocates against mediation in the context of domestic violence argue that violence creates an extreme imbalance of power between the parties by placing the victim in an impossible situation where he or she is more likely to feel pressured, coerced or intimidated into accepting an agreement against his or her interest. For instance, Rachel Field in her article[5] argues that patterns of violence are deeply entrenched, especially in cases of domestic violence, yet the perpetrators remain deceptively reasonable, and even charming in the way they portray themselves to others. This results in the victim being disadvantaged, as he or she has to assert his or her interests directly in the face of the perpetrator, while in the presence of a third-party mediator.[6] In my opinion, Field's position is limited in that it assumes that most perpetrators of domestic violence are scheming, manipulative and can put on a façade as and when they choose. Such façade by the perpetrator would potentially go far to convince the mediator that the parties are collaborative, the process is fair and the settlement is amicable. However, Field acknowledged that such perpetrators pose the threat of violent outburst, not just to the victim, but even the mediator. At the very least, this proves that not all perpetrators are able to put on a façade to manipulate the entire mediation process to their advantage. Nevertheless, examining Field's argument and the manner in which she portrays the perpetrator as deceptively reasonable, it can be suggested that the detrimental consequences to the victim is not solely because of the presence of a power imbalance, but also due to the lack of awareness of this power imbalance in the mediation. I personally agree that the lack of awareness is more pressing an issue, because practically speaking, it is unlikely for a mediator to allow for a settlement after the perpetrator has openly exerted elements of intimidation and coercion on the victim during the mediation. It is when the mediator is not aware of these actions that results in a real disadvantage to the victim.

In a similar vein, Lisa G. Lerman highlights that it is often assumed that parties have a safe space in mediation to air their grievances or to ask for change.[7,8] Instead, mediation could actually provide the coerced party a platform to exercise forms of non-physical control unbeknownst to the mediator. Other advocates against mediation in the context of domestic violence such as Margaret B. Drew take the same position.[9] Drew cautions that the collaborative setting in mediation could actually foster the power imbalance between the parties. For instance, in the context of domestic violence, there is likely a presence of signals such as specific looks, words or phrases that the perpetrator has been using to exercise control over the victim over a period of time. During the mediation, the perpetrator could abuse such signals to intimidate the victim to make concessions against his or her interest, appearing entirely reasonable and well organised while the victim struggles and could even behave inappropriately through the sessions.[10] To summarise, the essence of what these advocates are contending is that first, the power imbalance exists between the two parties because the victims continues to experience elements of intimidation and coercion during the mediation when dealing with the perpetrator. Second, this situation is exacerbated in a collaborative environment, where there may not be sufficient awareness of the extent of power imbalance between these parties. Accordingly, mediation is not appropriate for parties with a history of domestic abuse.

III. Measures aimed to manage power imbalances in mediation

Notably, there is an opposing school of thought — that mediation could still be an appropriate forum for resolving disputes in the context of domestic violence, because these power imbalances detrimental to the victim can be managed by measures such as screening, calling of frequent private caucuses, and if need be, shuttle mediations sessions. The starting point is an acknowledgement that not all parties with a history of domestic violence are suitable candidates for mediation. However, parties should first be evaluated individually before determining whether mediation is appropriate. This would also mitigate the lack of awareness (if any) that a mediator may have. Further, this position implicitly suggests that there are different degrees of power imbalances. As such, it may be premature to eliminate mediation as an option, without first turning to screening as a method to evaluate this degree of power imbalance present, and thereby determine if the power imbalance is manageable in a mediation or not.

The idea behind this contention is that first, power imbalances should not be presumed to exist behind every relationship with a history of domestic violence. Second, certain degrees of power imbalances are manageable in a mediation. To elaborate, Susan Landrum[11] cites the example of how some victims that have suffered through the ordeal of domestic violence have strong support systems in place that are effective in helping them through the difficult situation.[12] In such cases, these victims may have made promising recovery and are fully capable of participating in mediation despite their history of domestic violence. Landrum thus highlights the importance of evaluating whether couples should mediate on a case by case basis, where the history of domestic violence may not have significant bearing on the power imbalance between the parties.

Interestingly enough, there is a common consensus between the two different schools of thought that there are certain types of cases mediation will never be appropriate for. For instance, Amrita Narine, an advocate for the opposing school of thought, posits[13] that mediation may be inappropriate for scenarios of ongoing abuse, the perpetrator's use of threats or weapons, as well as the victim continuously putting the perpetrator's needs ahead of their own. This standard seems to be the threshold in deciding whether parties are suitable for mediation. Take the Tolman Screening Model[14] for instance, a questionnaire designed to provide guidance on which cases involving domestic violence are appropriate for mediation and which are not. According to the model, responses that indicate ongoing victim abuse and fear of the perpetrator, and/or the victim not feeling able to advocate his or her best interests, conclude that mediation is not appropriate. As we evaluate these cases that are filtered out as inappropriate for mediation, we see that all of them involve a severe imbalance of power between the victim and the perpetrator.

In my view, both schools of thought do agree on a standard, and rightly so — that mediation is inappropriate for cases with severe imbalance of power. Therefore, the key difference is that one group believes in the ability for mediation to manage up to a certain degree of power imbalance, while the other takes the stance that mediation should not be appropriate at all whenever there is a power imbalance. As aforementioned, the former group argues that mediation can utilise measures such as holding frequent private caucuses to check in on the parties, or even holding shuttle mediations. The rationale behind this is that private caucuses will benefit parties that are submissive and fear conflict (these characteristics are likely found in victims of domestic violence), as these parties may not be comfortable communicating their feelings in front of the more dominant party. Moreover, Narine posits that private caucuses are essential for mediators to check in with the victims at points of agreement or disagreement, to ensure that he or she is not intimidated or coerced into making those decisions.[15] In situations where the victim is unable or unwilling to directly face the perpetrator, there is also the option of shuttle mediation, where the mediator will move back and forth between private sessions for both parties. Being in different rooms, or having different mediation sessions altogether, will likely bring more comfort to the victim, but more importantly, it significantly decreases the chance of intimidation or coercion to occur.[16] In addition, Landrum also suggests that the mediator can think of screening as an ongoing process in the mediation, rather than a one-time process. With this mindset, the mediator is more likely to pick up subtle indicators or sometimes even overt signs that the perpetrator is still intimidating or coercing the victim to get what he or she wants in the mediation.[17]

Conversely, this approach also has its weaknesses. First, Lerman submits that these screening criteria are often amorphous and not consistently applied.[18] Indeed, I agree that this issue is true to a large extent. It is impossible to consistently apply a criterion. Even if we filter out the cases not appropriate for mediation based on the standard of "severe imbalance of power" as aforementioned, what exactly does this mean? At the end of the day, it still requires the exercise of discretion in making this decision.

Likewise, Field submits that for this reason a mediator's genuine belief that they are capable of redressing power imbalances in all cases not filtered out may be unfounded.[19] Moreover, we must not forget that in the context of domestic violence, the mediator also has many other prominent concerns such as diffusing hostility. As such, it is too risky for this approach to essentially rely solely on the mediator's ability to assess the circumstances accurately.

Nevertheless, I personally prefer the approaches by Landrum and Narine. Firstly, the approach encapsulates measures that determine the degree of power imbalance between the parties including measures taken pre-mediation such as screening. Moreover, these methods do reduce the extent of unawareness of the power imbalance in mediation. Secondly, measures taken during mediation can ensure that the power imbalances are effectively managed. While I largely agree that this approach is weak in that screening is amorphous and may never be consistent, I believe that Landrum's suggestion for mediators to consider screening as an ongoing process would help alleviate the unwelcome scenario where the mediator is unable to accurately assess the extent of power imbalance, as mediators can constantly assess the victims' well-being. Furthermore, there is still the option for mediators to call off the mediation at any stage where it is apparent that the extent of power imbalance is too severe.

IV. Public policy concerns

In addition, mediating family disputes where there is a history of domestic violence could potentially send the wrong message to society as a matter of public policy. The core of this argument is that mediation does not require the perpetrator to take responsibility for his or her abusive actions.[20] In my opinion, this reasoning is logical based on the given circumstances, since there is no judge, there is no "judgement" per se in a mediation. In the absence of a "judgement", it potentially sends a message to society that domestic violence is tolerable, and that the courts have to a certain extent failed to treat domestic violence as a crime.[21] Moreover, mediation is meant to be held in a confidential environment, with some even coining the dispute resolution mechanism as "private justice behind closed doors".[22] Thus, dealing with issues that encompass domestic violence in mediation instead of public civil divorce proceedings, or even criminal prosecution, actually brings the scrutiny of domestic violence outside of the public eye. This results in significant policy concerns as it potentially reinforces the idea that domestic violence is a private or family problem. At the same time, given that mediation is a collaborative environment where parties gather to find a resolution for what many see as a dispute between both parties, this could even suggest that both parties are responsible for the domestic violence. For these reasons, Landrum argues that these negative repercussions could manifest in even more detrimental forms if not adequately addressed, such as creating more potential violence against victims in the future.[23]

While I agree that all the aforementioned policy concerns are valid, I am of the opinion that these concerns are not as severe as described, because these concerns all seem to revolve around the assumption that domestic violence is the core subject to be resolved during the mediation. On the contrary, domestic violence is actually the background context behind the core subjects in dispute, such as child custody issues, issues related to separation or divorce. Therefore, even in the scenario where a victim goes through with mediation and manages to resolve the issues, he or she is not necessarily precluded from making a report of domestic violence to the authorities nor filing a civil claim against the perpetrator. On this subject, I acknowledge that in allowing for mediation to directly manage and deal with the impacts of domestic violence, it continues to send a message that to a certain extent, issues revolving around domestic violence can be resolved behind closed doors.

In contrast, some mediation advocates argue that the mediation process is particularly beneficial for victims of domestic violence, as it provides the tools that they require to support their interests and even enhance their safety. For instance, Sandra Zaher asserts that mediation can empower the victims of domestic violence by enabling them to speak in their own voice, and to even assert their own interests, perhaps for the first time.[24] Similarly, Rimelspach considers that mediation provides victims a future-oriented process, focused on where they are moving forward with their lives, as whole independent individuals.[25] Further, Rimelspach also cites a study[26] conducted in Ontario by Professor Desmond Ellis that found that mediations actually correlated with a greater reduction in domestic abuse than lawyer-assisted settlements. While I can see how it is possible that the collaborative aspect of mediation can potentially be used as a tool to end the cycle of violence and even empower the victims by enabling them to speak up for their own interests, I take the position that these benefits only apply on a case-by-case basis. In my view, it really depends on the victim and the circumstances behind the abuse. To elaborate, if the abuse was too recent or too severe, the victim may not be able to effectively fight for his or her interests, even when provided with the platform to do so. Conversely, if the victim had strong support systems to encourage and aid the victim's recovery, mediation might have that empowerment effect as aforementioned.

Accordingly, I lean towards the view that neither the concern of sending the wrong message to society, nor the potential empowering benefits that mediation may bring, are significant enough to tilt the scales in determining whether mediation is appropriate in the context of domestic violence on the basis of public policy.

V. Evaluation and suggestions

All in all, after the discussion behind the contentious issue of power imbalance, I personally subscribe to the approach that mediation is beneficial as an option for dispute resolution even in the context of domestic violence. I do recognise the many drawbacks and risks that come from an imbalance of power between the parties due to the impact of domestic violence, yet I believe that the presence of measures and mechanisms within the mediation and pre-mediation process is sufficient to manage these issues. Hence, in my view, the option of mediation should not be immediately eliminated from the onset in the context of domestic violence. In any case, mediators have the power to call off the mediation at any stage when it is apparent that the extent of power imbalance is too severe.

Finally, I believe it is beneficial to set out a framework on how to approach mediation in the context of domestic violence, based on the suggestions by Landrum and Narine. The first step is for both parties to go through a screening process. This is necessary to determine if the power imbalance is too severe to be appropriate for parties to go through mediation. This also indicates that it is not only important to evaluate the victim, but also the perpetrator of the domestic violence. This will help to define as accurately as possible the extent of power imbalance between the parties. In this regard, I do not think the use of models such as the Tolman screening model alone is sufficient. Such models can be used as a starting point, but it is suggested that the mediator must personally screen the parties individually, on a case-by-case basis, so that he or she can make the decision with the benefit of a mediator's expertise as to whether mediation is appropriate for that particular case. Second, after the screening process, if the mediator considers that notwithstanding the history of domestic violence, parties could give mediation a shot, then the mediator should go into the mediation consciously aware of the history and the potential risks. Thirdly, in being mindful of these risks, the mediator must continuously evaluate the parties to ensure that the extent of power imbalance does not adversely affect the victim's ability to act for his or her interests. The mediator can do so by constantly taking measures such as the calling of private caucuses, or even shuttle meditation. Finally, the mediator must always be alive to the option of calling off the mediation at any stage if he or she feels that the power imbalance will adversely affect the victim's ability to act in his or her own interest. With such measures in place, I strongly believe that the interests of victims of domestic violence can be protected and served at the same time by using mediation as the forum of dispute resolution.

Lessons from Transformative Mediation and How It Can Benefit Singapore's Mediation Landscape

Yap Shi Kai

I. Introduction

As the Singapore Convention on Mediation[1] strengthens Singapore's offerings as a leading global dispute resolution hub and promotes the use of mediation to resolve cross-border commercial disputes, it is important to consider how mediation in Singapore should evolve to encompass the best practices of different mediation models.

While a myriad of models has been adopted in different dispute resolution settings,[2] facilitative mediation is currently the model of choice in Singapore — it is utilised by both the Singapore Mediation Centre and Singapore International Mediation Centre whose panels of mediators are accordingly trained in using this approach.[3] The facilitative, or interest-based model traces its origins to the Harvard Negotiation Project[4] and attempts to shift the parties from a rights-based, positional approach to an approach that focuses on the real interests of the parties. The mediator is described as taking a "back-seat", neither offering an evaluation of the case nor recommending solutions to the parties. This approach is widely adopted in the United States, Hong Kong and Australia, among others.[5]

Transformative mediation was first introduced by Robert A. Baruch Bush and Joseph P. Folger in their seminal book *The Promise of Mediation* in 1994.[6] Transformative mediation utilises a social constructivist and communicative view of human conflict,[7] with the goal of conflict transformation by transforming how parties relate to each other and empowering them to enable the healing and reconciliation of relationships. Although transformative mediation has been criticised for its dogmatism and weak doctrinal basis,[8] it nevertheless articulates a clear set of principles for mediators to follow. Transformative mediation has also been found to have high user satisfaction and long-lasting effects, as its large-scale implementation with the United States Postal Services showed.[9]

As Lee and Teh note, the distinction between different mediation models is blurred in practice and mediators often describe themselves as having a "toolbox" of skills.[10] Hence, this chapter explores how concepts from transformative mediation can add to the Singaporean mediator's toolbox and create a more pluralist mediation landscape for different types of disputes.

II. Key characteristics of transformative mediation

This section describes some key characteristics of Transformative Mediation and suggests ways for practical application by mediators.

A. *Reversing the vicious cycle: recognition follows empowerment*

Bush and Folger argue that conflict creates a vicious cycle of weakness and self-absorption. Weakness in disputes robs parties of their autonomy and results in suspicion and alienation from others, leading to more hostile stances and eventually more weakness and self-absorption.[11] A key priority of transformative mediation is hence reversing this cycle, and this occurs through recognition, which follows empowerment.

Empowerment refers to enabling the parties to describe their own issues and seek their own solutions to problems (as opposed to having the issues and solutions defined by the mediator). Empowerment is achieved when parties grow calmer, clearer, more confident and more decisive, regaining their sense of strength and being able to take control of their situation.[12] Recognition is the evocation in individuals of acknowledgement and empathy for the situation and problems of others. Recognition is achieved when, given some degree of empowerment, parties "voluntarily choose to become more open, attentive, sympathetic, and responsive to the situation of the other party, thereby expanding their perspective to include an appreciation for another's situation".[13]

An important observation is that empowerment tends to precede recognition, since people in conflict rarely display much generosity towards each other until their own needs are dealt with.[14] The role of transformative mediators is to call attention to opportunities for empowerment and recognition, although they should not lead parties towards a particular outcome. This process is not unlike facilitative mediation[15] although the focus is markedly different.

The focus on "recognition" in transformative mediation stands in contrast to the heuristic "separate people from the problem", which implies a need to identify the substantive or legal issues, as opposed to the relationship issues at hand.[16] Therefore, a transformative mediator would support the parties if they wished to dwell at length on emotional or relationship matters, understanding that it is a crucial component of transforming their conflict. Although "empowerment" resembles the respect for "party autonomy" found in facilitative models, transformative mediators take this to a far higher degree by reflecting the parties' sentiments back to them in the form of "summaries" and "check-ins", and refraining from process interventions even if the parties "back-slide" into an earlier topic.[17] The mediator also listens closely for any empowerment or recognition shifts and encourages their willing efforts at mutual perspective-taking at every opportunity.

On a practical level, the mediator would seek to empower the parties at every opportunity by encouraging them to take control of the session and decide what they want to talk about. Whereas a summary from a facilitative mediator might choose to focus on their common and shared interests, a transformative mediator would instead organise and condense what the parties have talked about into topics of discussion[18] regardless of whether the topics were common or potentially divisive. The mediator would also seek to recognise the party's empowerment and recognition shifts at every opportunity, in the form of a summary or "check-in" to call attention to it. A question as simple as "I'm not sure I understand fully what you've said, can you talk a bit more about that?" and then subsequently asking the other party whether the information might alter his or her view of the other disputant or the conflict in general, could encourage both parties to recognise the empowerment shifts that have occurred in the discussion.

B. *Emotions are not taboo: allow and be responsive to parties' expressions of emotions*

As Bush and Folger put it, there are facts in the feelings:[19] whereas facilitative or settlement mediators may view the expression of strong emotions as a hindrance and try to lead the parties towards common interests, transformative mediators consider the expression of emotions an integral part of the conflict process, as it brings forth important opportunities for empowerment and recognition. Frustration, for example, could indicate uncertainty about one's options, while anger could stem from a lack of understanding about the other's personal situation. In such instances, the mediator could use these expressions of emotion as an opportunity for greater recognition by one party of the "other" and encourage empowerment or recognition shifts. Where highly emotive situations are often characterised by tense emotions and the lack of listening to the other party, the mediator can utilise reflection by mirroring back to the speaker what the mediator believes the speaker has just expressed, capturing both the substance and emotional tone of what the speaker has said.[20] Reflection allows the other party to hear the original party's emotions without feeling attacked, while allowing the original party to hear himself or herself, as a kind of "conversation with himself or herself".

Similarly, Mayer has argued that it is counter-productive to equate respect with not showing anger, especially when parties in dispute resolution often do not respect each other to begin with.[21] Therefore, stifling expression of strong emotions or blunting true opinions or feelings would contribute to avoiding, minimising or making light of essential differences. Without an acknowledgement of the essential differences between the parties, doubt creation — which is key to the facilitative model — cannot work as well.[22]

Perhaps counter-intuitively, the expression of strong emotions can lead parties to greater clarity. Anger can reduce the effect of confirmation bias and allow parties to become more open-minded than parties who do not express their anger or suppress their anger.[23] Furthermore, they could subsequently be in a detail-oriented state of mind in order to rebut errors or inconsistencies, giving them a greater sense of control of the situation,[24] a clear empowerment shift as predicted by Bush and Folger.

On a practical level, Bush and Folger suggest that when parties express emotion, the mediator should not wait until it is over and then go with issue discussion. Apart from reflection, the mediator can ask both parties to describe their feelings and the situations and events that give rise to them. These descriptions of the facts behind the feelings very often reveal specific points that the parties are struggling to deal with, both to gain control over their situation and to understand and be understood by the other party.[25] Therefore, the mediator has a crucial role in uncovering the messages behind the emotions. It is further suggested that short of abusive, bullying or threatening behaviour, the mediator can be more tolerant of expressions of strong emotion as an opportunity for empowerment and recognition.

C. *A more-than-settlement orientation*

The emphasis on reaching a settlement was clear in the development of mediation in Singapore, as one of the express goals was to ease judicial caseload.[26] Therefore, mediation is often evaluated on its settlement rate, perhaps due to its initial comparison, and indeed competition, with other forms of dispute resolution. The emphasis on efficient settlements has led to forms of mediation such as Settlement Mediation[a] and this would have influenced mediators in Singapore even as they proclaim to be facilitative mediators. Bush and Folger argue that an over-emphasis on settlement neglects the key strengths of mediation that separate it from other forms of dispute resolution, namely party empowerment and conflict transformation.[27] While academics and practitioners often misunderstand transformative mediation in the sense that it does not view settlement as important,[28] transformative mediators have a long-term view of conflict and consider other indicators of success as well, such as conflict transformation. While settlement is important, it should not come under

[a]In which the mediators become a process driver of positional bargaining.

pressure or the direction of the mediator and should be what the parties arrive at on their own.[29] As Bush and Folger note, the mediator's intervention is only one point within a longer time frame, and even accepting the terms of the settlement is not the same as carrying them out, or a guarantee that the conflict will not resurface. Hence, it would be a more valuable accomplishment if parties can establish a firmer relationship, based on greater empowerment and recognition, as their interaction continues beyond the session. In the long term, the transformative style may also heighten disputants' perceptions of interpersonal bias and reduce the perceptions of structural bias,[30] reducing the likelihood of future conflict.

Furthermore, Mayer has criticised the singular view that interest-based negotiation, as adopted by facilitative mediators, will aid towards settlement. As he noted, some problems are purely positional with no win-win outcome.[31] In a genuinely distributive situation, where there are serious vulnerabilities, people might feel mistrustful and unwilling to disclose their real interests. Paradoxically, a focus on empowerment and recognition would allow parties to look past the purely positional negotiations whereas the interest-based model would not work.

On a practical level, the mediator has an important role to play in setting expectations of the parties. In the opening statement, it is suggested that the mediator frames formal agreement or settlement as merely one possible outcome of the process and describes other outcomes that can be equally important. He or she can emphasise that the session can be successful if new insights are reached, choices are clarified, or if new understandings of each other's views are achieved.[32] The mediator should refrain from rushing the parties to settlement, and instead focus on empowerment and recognition of the parties.

D. *The parties know best and have what it takes*

Although the facilitative mediator is supposed to withhold from commenting on the merits of the parties' case or suggesting options, mediators in Singapore continue to overwhelmingly do so. In a post-mediation survey conducted by the Singapore Mediation Centre,[33] 79% of mediators evaluated the merits of one's case, while 85% of mediators suggested settlement options. It is unclear whether this is a cultural phenomenon, where parties respect the mediator's authority and expect them to give advice[34] or an indication of the more proactive role of Singaporean mediators in general.

While cultural differences must be respected, Bush and Folger suggest that the parties' autonomy and ability should never be supplanted by an overzealous mediator. The transformative practice includes the refusal of the mediator to be judgemental about the parties' views on and decisions about their situation and each other,[35] as well as a positive view of the parties' fundamental competence and their ability to deal with their own situation on their own terms. Crucially, the mediator sees the parties, even in their worst moments, as only being *temporarily* disabled, weakened or self-absorbed, and seeks to move them from weakness to strength through empowerment and recognition.

On a practical level, it is suggested that the mediator refrains from making assumptions about the parties, especially the assumption that he knows the merits of their case better than them, or imputes negative intentions to them. The mediator should catch, pull back and suspend judgement instead of exercising it,[36] and support (but not supplant) the parties' decisions. The mediator should look for opportunities for empowerment and recognition when parties are temporarily unable to be collaborative. Of course, this involves a paradigm shift in the mindset of a mediator and is arguably the hardest to change.

III. Limitations: consideration of the Asian context

Even as Singapore endeavours to become a key mediation hub and attract foreign parties to mediate, it cannot ignore the local and regional cultural trends and behaviour that lie beneath. In this section, a few cultural limitations to the application of transformative practices are discussed.

A. *Reluctance to air dirty laundry in public*

Lee and Teh have noted the cultural importance of "face"[37] as parties in Asia tend to be reluctant to "air dirty laundry in public", even if they stridently disagree with each other. Parties may be reluctant to be honest and express their emotions in a joint session, preferring to use private sessions or caucuses to lay out their grievances and anger.[38] This could lead to parties refusing to be open and honest in revealing their concerns or interests and hamper progress in the mediation.

As a practical adjustment, the mediator should use the private session as an opportunity to empower and recognise the parties' concerns and emotions. Instead of suppressing them or advising them to not express these emotions, mediators can empower the parties to express these grievances in a way that is face-saving for the other party[39] by reframing the heated words in a positive-negative-positive framework, for instance. As Ting-Tooney noted, "face" is a complex concept that is not just about not embarrassing someone; it could also include face-giving in sharing one's honest thoughts and opinion, albeit in a more palatable way.[40]

B. *Mediator authority*

In Asian contexts, including Singapore, the mediator is often expected to be someone of greater standing when compared to disputants.[41] Therefore, the parties are more likely to follow the authority of the mediator and may expect the mediator to give advice and make decisions, even perceiving the mediator as ineffective and untrustworthy when he fails to do so.

This may come at odds with some of the principles of transformative mediation, which focuses on empowering the parties to make their own decisions and prevents the mediator from giving advice or directing the parties.

It is suggested, perhaps counter-intuitively, that the mediator focus this respect and authority that he or she is given on empowering and recognising the efforts and ideas of the parties. The mediator may need to offer cogent reasons why he or she is refraining from advising on the merits of the parties' cases and reassure the parties of their ability to be their best advocate. It may come in a statement like, "From my experience, it is best when parties work out the solution together, instead of the mediator doing so".

C. *Practical difficulties*

Some academics have opined that transformative mediation may not be appropriate for disputes involving victims of Post-Traumatic Stress

Disorder[42] or disputes with a stark power imbalance since mediators would not be able to prevent one party from taking advantage of the other.[43] Furthermore, transformative mediation is said to demand a greater time investment than other mediation models[44] since the processes of empowerment and recognition could involve significant time and backsliding, as Bush and Folger acknowledge.

Without further empirical research on these limitations of transformative mediation, it is suggested that transformative mediation be applied to specific types of disputes. Transformative strategies could find its niche in long-term disputes where parties have repeated interactions and the capacity to grow. Alexander has noted that transformative mediation processes are often used where people have strong views and emotions such as in environmental and community conflicts, victim-offender matters and disputes involving family members.[45] The United States Postal Services REDRESS program, which utilised the transformative mediation model, achieved high satisfaction rates and greatly reduced the number of workplace disputes thereafter, showing its potential in a workplace setting.[46]

IV. Conclusion

This chapter has attempted to give a broad overview of how lessons from transformative mediation can aid in developing further strategies for mediators in Singapore. While the facilitative and interest-based models have been taught to students and mediators since the inception of modern mediation in Singapore, relatively little attention has been given to other, more obscure (at least in Singapore) forms of mediation practices. Furthermore, heuristics and frameworks such as the interest-option distinction and "separating the people from the problem" have been commonly accepted without question in Singapore. This chapter hopes to encourage further discussion and debate on the justifications for various mediation techniques in Singapore and re-ignite some of the ideological and practical reasons for why we do what we do. While it is unrealistic to expect an ideological shift in the mediation models that have been established in Singapore for decades, it is hoped that this chapter will at least contribute to the Singaporean mediator's toolbox in preparing him or her for a more pluralist mediation landscape.

"Paiseh!" — Apologies, Restorative Justice and Criminal Mediation in Singapore

Benedict Koh Yen Hin

I. Introduction

"Paiseh!"[1] This Singlish[2] phrase for apology is a common aspect of Singapore's colloquialism,[3] enjoying application in various situations — from young children apologising to appease bullies during a playground fight,[4] to people avoiding physical clashes by apologising to hooligans at the onset of staring incidents.[5]

Past commentators have explored the instrumentality of apologies in mediation.[6] The existing literature discusses the forms of apologies[7] and their impacts on the mediation's dynamics.[8]

However, the conversation has been limited to discussions outside the context of criminal mediation in Singapore, a growing area of mediation that has received little academic coverage.[9] Contrary to presumptions of universality,[10] observers have recognised that principles of mediation should not be applied wholesale to every given context[11] but should be, where required, adapted to specific cultural[12] and situational[13] conditions.

Hence, this chapter aims to expand the discourse by exploring the utility and limitations of apologies in promoting restorative justice in the context of criminal mediation, through the lens of Singapore's culture.

II. Short answer

Prima facie, apologies help promote restorative justice in the context of criminal mediation due to their inherent benefits, including the restoration of the parties' balance of power and reconciliation of the giver (respondent) with the wider community.

However, these benefits are subject to limitations, including parties' aversion towards apologising sincerely and the existence of incentives and cultural reasons for parties to abuse the mediation process.

III. Criminal mediation in Singapore

Before delving into apologies in relation to criminal mediation in Singapore, one must first recognise that the term "criminal mediation" has been interpreted inconsistently by various commentators to be interchangeable with other processes,[14] such as Criminal Case Resolution (CCR).[15]

Therefore, we must demarcate the scope of criminal mediation for discussion.

A. *Overview of schemes for managing and settling criminal cases*

In Singapore, there are three schemes tailored towards resolving criminal cases. These are criminal mediation;[16] the Criminal Case Management System (CCMS);[17] and CCR.[18] While this research study delves into the criminal mediation scheme, it is worth noting its key distinguishing factors.[19]

The CCMS and CCR are tailored towards case management,[20] where parties streamline the legal issues to save time and resources by weeding out "cracked trials", [21] or cases which would result in a guilty plea early on in the trial.[22] However, these do not resolve the underlying dispute between the accused and the victim(s).

B. *Criminal mediation*

(1) *Features of criminal mediation*

Unlike victim-offender mediation,[23] where the respondent's guilt has been established, the matter would have yet to go to trial. This means the complainant may drop the charges without investigations formally commencing,[24] should the parties come to a settlement.

This process is available for offences normally prosecuted under the private prosecution process,[25] pursuant to Sections 151–153 of the Criminal Procedure Code (CPC),[26] read with Section 15 of the Community Mediation Centres Act (CMCA).[27] Unlike regular criminal cases,[28] where the Attorney-General's Chambers (AGC) officers perform the prosecution,[29] the complainant leads the prosecution, enjoying the discretion to terminate the proceedings.[30]

(2) *Restorative justice*

Unlike CCMS and CCR, criminal mediation has the goal of *resolving* the *underlying dispute or conflict* between the parties involved.

The central theme is restorative justice,[31] through which parties collaborate to focus on the past harm and how best to prevent it in future.[32] The goal is that parties would come to an amicable settlement with the respondent's guilt still not pronounced,[33] in order to achieve the following[34]:

(a) helping both parties achieve closure, regarding the past;
(b) helping the respondent be accountable for his actions and, where applicable, make restitution to the complainant; and
(c) preventing future recurrence of the offence by, *inter alia*, agreeing to arrangements to achieve this.[35]

IV. Understanding the apology in general

The apology is regarded to mean "to acknowledge and express regret for a fault without defence",[36] encompassing three core elements as laid out by Schneider,[37] namely, (a) acknowledgement;[38] (b) affect;[39] and (c) vulnerability.[40]

A. *Acknowledgement*

Acknowledgement encompasses the *recognition* of an injury damaging the bonds between the complainant and respondent due to the violation of a relational or moral norm, damaging the respondent's social bonds and bringing into question his membership in the community.[41]

Here, this recognition of the injury entails the respondent being *personally accountable* for his role as the offending party.

B. *Affect*

Affect requires the Respondent to be *personally visibly affected* by his actions. The oft cited anecdote concerns former US President Bill Clinton's "apology" following his sexual affair with Monica Lewinsky,[42] where he was perceived to have not displayed any form of regret or remorse.[43]

C. *Vulnerability*

Vulnerability entails the respondent offering the apology despite knowing that the complainant might decline it. This marks a shift in power,[44] with the respondent being open to the possibility that the complainant would instead choose to pursue the case instead of accepting the apology, thereby placing the respondent in a state of vulnerability.[45]

V. Where apologies promote restorative justice

The value of apology in promoting restorative justice has been recognised in the context of victim-offender mediation.[46] Arguably, there is such similar value in criminal mediation, even though the respondent's guilt would not have been legally established.[47]

A. *Working presumption*

The working presumption is that the apology offered possesses all three elements of acknowledgement, affect and vulnerability. Here, the fact that the respondent's guilt has not been legally established is not an obstacle, because for the parties to even proceed to criminal mediation, the Magistrate must first examine the complainant on oath[48] and determine whether there is sufficient reason for the complaint to proceed.[49]

Thus, this signifies that there must exist an *underlying conflict* between the parties to the mediation, even if the actions pertaining or giving rise to this conflict might not be in contravention of the law.

B. *Reconciling the parties*

The apology has been recognised for its ability to empower the victim.[50] The apology is acknowledged for restoring, at least partially, the parties' moral balance of power.[51] Such empowerment also applies in Singapore's criminal mediation context.

(1) *Reversing the parties' roles — restoring the parties' moral balance of power*

The apology is instrumental in reversing the parties' roles through the exchange of shame and power between parties. This helps restore moral balance because the conflict has disrupted the parties' abilities to deal with each other on an equal footing.

Therefore, the apology impacts both the complainant and respondent simultaneously, working when both parties are *ad idem*.[52]

(a) Individual impact on the complainant (receiver)

In receiving the apology, based on the view that the complainant suffers from a victimised loss of self-concept,[53] the complainant is receiving reparation for his lowered self-esteem, pain and vulnerability. This helps the complainant release his resentment for the moral harm done,[54] in turn beginning the *healing* process.

Furthermore, in being offered the apology, applying the element of vulnerability,[55] the complainant attains a position of greater power, with the discretion to decide whether to accept the apology.

Overarchingly, receiving the apology kickstarts the *empowerment* process for the complainant.[56] Through receiving the respondent's acknowledgement of the error of his ways, the complainant feels validated, reinforcing the foundation for recovery.[57]

(b) Individual impact on the respondent (giver)

Conversely, the respondent, in offering a sincere apology, puts himself at the complainant's mercy, since he is uncertain if the complainant will accept the apology.[58] Consequently, the offer of the apology signifies that the respondent is taking responsibility for his actions and their consequences.[59]

(c) Collective impact on the parties — restoration of relationship

Through the concurrent giving of the respondent's apology and the complainant's acceptance, both parties deny their self-serving and self-preserving tendencies.[60]

In turn, a shift in balance of power takes place, accomplished when the respondent begins taking responsibility for his actions, simultaneously decreasing the complainant's own burden of responsibility,[61] leading to an *empowerment* of the complainant.

(2) *Strengthening of parties' future relationship*

Furthermore, apologies serve as the foundation for parties to strengthen their future relationship.[62] Where the apology is authentic and fueled by the respondent's sincere wish to make amends, this restores the essential element of trust between the parties.[63]

With this trust in place, the parties would then better understand each other and work out arrangements to avoid future occurrences of the offence in question.[64] This represents a big step towards restorative justice, with this renewed mutual trust serving as the lens through which the parties view their future relationship.[65]

C. *Reconciliation with the wider community*

Overarchingly, the apology also serves to restore the relationship between the respondent and the community at large,[66] by showing that the respondent is ready and willing to abide by societal norms, which serve as the community's moral fabric.[67]

Given that criminal offences are widely regarded as morally injurious to society,[68] the apology could mark the respondent's commitment to change one's ways as a positive step towards healing the moral bond between the respondent and society.

VI. Obstacles to achieving restorative justice with apologies

However, despite the restorative benefits the apology has, it is far from being a perfect solution to help mediating parties come to a resolution. Past literature has explained (a) parties' aversion to apologising, and, even where utilised, (b) the inherent limitations of the apology in the general mediation context, with reference to attributes such as cultural, psychological and legal concerns.[69]

Likewise, such obstacles are also faced in the promotion of restorative justice in criminal mediation in Singapore. This is because the aforementioned working presumption that all apologies fulfil the three elements as laid out by Schneider[70] will not hold.

On a preliminary note, it is widely recognised that Singaporeans tend to live by the "*kiasu*" mentality[71] — colloquially understood to refer to a mindset of extreme competitiveness, stemming from the fear of losing out.[72]

This encompasses a fear of losing in both (a) the criminal mediation proceedings; and (b) further opportunities in one's career, stemming from conviction of a criminal offence.[73]

A. *Aversion due to fear of losing "face"*

Parties in Singapore proceedings could be averse to even giving an apology, because (a) they associate apologising with a loss of "face"; and (b) might not provide a full apology fulfilling the three elements, so as to not admit liability.

The fear of loss of "face" stems from psychological and cultural reasons, including apathy and pride, and is further bolstered by a lack of ownership of the parties over the mediation itself, given that the parties might not have voluntarily wished to go to mediation in the first place.

(1) *Psychology and culture*

Firstly, in determining the postulated loss of "face" from apologising, one should note that this fear typically stems from the parties' pride and egocentricity.[74] Such attributes square neatly with the local mindset,[75] best highlighted by the oft cited Not-in-my-backyard (NIMBY) syndrome.[76]

This reflects a general sense of apathy towards the situations of other people, and consequent pride stemming from their perception of possessing the moral high ground. Since apologising to the other party has already been established to result in the "lowering" of the giver's standing as regards the parties in question, therein lies the difficulty of even getting the respondent to apologise in the first place.

This mentality flies in the face of a true apology and the success of the criminal mediation, due to its direct contradiction of the elements of acknowledgement[77] and affect.[78]

Acknowledgement could be absent, due to the parties' inability to empathise with the other party's situation. This stems from the lifestyle which the average Singaporean is used to, where the NIMBY syndrome plays a pivotal role in ingraining an apathetic mindset, resulting in an increased likelihood of acknowledgement being absent.

Consequently, the element of affect is likely absent. Due to the respondent's lack of acknowledgement for the injury caused to the complainant,[79] it is unlikely that the respondent would show genuine concern or regret for having caused such injury, since that would not be what the respondent subjectively believes.

In any case, the above likely holds true due to institutional factors, since the respondent would likely believe he or she has no fault, especially since the respondent's guilt has not been definitively pronounced.[80]

As such, unlike what the complainant believes, from the viewpoint of the respondent, the respondent has not upset the moral balance of power between the parties,[81] and hence should not take any unnecessary steps to restore such balance.

(2) *Lack of ownership over the mediation*

Secondly, these difficulties are bolstered by the parties' possible lack of ownership over the mediation, since they might not even have voluntarily wished to participate in criminal mediation.

Furthermore, this signifies a lack of ownership over the restorative justice process. This is concerning, due to the inherent value of parties' self-determination[82] as being of core essence to the process's success.[83] Without voluntariness, the issues are two-fold — firstly, there exists a lower likelihood of sincere apology; and, a lower likelihood of acceptance of the apology.

The potential lack of voluntariness exists due to criminal mediation's status as a form of mandatory mediation.[84] Under Section 15(1) CMCA,[85] the Magistrate has the discretion to refer parties to criminal mediation *even without their consent*. Furthermore, should the case proceed to trial, the Magistrate could consider the parties' non-attendance at these sessions as disadvantageous factors against the respective parties.[86] These indicate a *coercion* of the parties to attend criminal mediation against their will.[87]

Therefore, the added difficulty is that parties might feel that they have lost "face" by even attending the sessions.[88]

B. *Legal concerns*

Legal concerns also tend to weigh on parties' minds, resulting in parties' tendency to use the apology tactically. Firstly, parties are averse to making an apology because they are afraid of admitting legal liability. Secondly, even where apologies are given, parties tend to make them tactically, rather than wholeheartedly.

(1) *Fear of admitting to legal liability*

Parties tend to underestimate the impact of making an apology, due to the common assumption that expressions of empathy in mediation are synonymous with admitting to one's fault or guilt.[89]

Such guarded mentalities towards criminal mediation fly in the face of mediation's ideals — where openness and collaboration among the parties is of greatest value,[90] with a view to achieving win-win outcomes.[91]

These mentalities also originate from the parties' lawyers, who tend to be ingrained with the values of Singapore's adversarial legal system,[92] espoused in the dichotomous "win-lose" approach towards disputes.[93] This could result in parties potentially shunning the ideals of collaborative dispute resolution.

Hence, despite mediators' strong reassurances that the mediation discussions are confidential and without prejudice,[94] the systemically ingrained mentalities of the parties and their legal representatives would tend to result in parties not being forthcoming with their apologies.

(2) *Tactical apologies*

(a) Incentive for parties to use tactical apologies

Flowing from the parties' tendency to approach the mediation sessions with an adversarial mindset, this issue is further compounded when seen in light of Singaporean's "*kiasi*" mindset — loosely translated to mean a "fear of death".[95] This extends to the fear of criminal sanctions and court proceedings, which are viewed in our Asian/Confucian context to be the equivalent of a "death sentence" in Singapore's increasingly competitive environment[96] where a criminal conviction could both potentially spell the end of one's career prospects;[97] and bring dishonour to one's family.[98]

Therefore, given that the complainant has the discretion to drop all criminal charges against the respondent via a settlement,[99] it would be in the respondent's personal interest to build rapport with the complainant, even if one does not sincerely mean it.

(b) How parties use tactical apologies

Turning towards the issue of tactical apologies, which refer to apologies used for an underlying competitive purpose, lawyers use apologies as a means of gaining credibility during negotiations[100] to build rapport with the complainant.

In so doing, the respondent, motivated by the desire to have the complainant drop criminal charges and demand less restitution, essentially seeks to utilise any means necessary to get the complainant to relinquish his legal rights,[101] even where the respondent does not intend to act in good faith in restoring the parties' relationship after the mediation.

C. *Manipulation of complainant into acceptance*

Conversely, the complainant could also face additional undue pressure to accept the apology offered, even where such acceptance might not be wholehearted, as gathered through past studies of victims' responses to apologies in the context of victim-offender mediation,[102] where victims have found it difficult to rebuff apologies, because they felt like there was no other option.[103]

Transposing these concerns to Singapore's criminal mediation scene, this likely applies particularly in relational disputes,[104] due to the societal upholding of the value of interpersonal relations. Although, paradoxically, the purpose of criminal mediation of relational disputes is to restore the parties' relationship, there is a greater chance of complainants feeling unduly pressured into accepting apologies, due to the perceived need to preserve the relationship, even against their will.

VII. Conclusion

This chapter has sought to show how the apology helps promote restorative justice in criminal mediation, due to its potential utilisation for helping to restore the parties' relationship. However, there exist limitations in the form of parties' aversion towards apologising sincerely, coupled with incentives and cultural reasons for parties to abuse the mediation process to achieve their desired outcomes.

While past literature has suggested that mediation is rarely abused in Singapore,[105] tactical advocacy and undue manipulation cannot be ruled out especially since mediating parties usually come into the discussion only because there has been a breakdown in the relationship.[106] Nevertheless, we must temper these theoretical postulations with empirical evidence, which is presently scarce.

Endnotes

Chapter 1 The Need for Mediation Advocacy Standards in Singapore

1. Charmaine Ng, "New body set to raise Singapore's profile as dispute resolution hub", *The Straits Times* (27 June 2019) <https://www.straitstimes.com/singapore/new-body-set-to-raise-singapores-profile-as-dispute-resolution-hub#:~:text=A%20new%20group%20to%20promote,international%20arbitration%20and%20dispute%20resolution> (accessed 31 March 2020); Calvin Yang, "Parliament: New Bill aims to strengthen Singapore's offerings as dispute resolution hub", *The Straits Times* (6 January 2020) <https://www.straitstimes.com/politics/parliament-new-bill-aims-to-strengthen-singapores-offerings-as-dispute-resolution-hub> (accessed 31 March 2020); Calvin Yang, "New Bill to boost Singapore's global role as a mediation hub", *The Straits Time* (8 January 2020), online: <https://www.straitstimes.com/singapore/new-bill-to-boost-spores-global-role-as-mediation-hub> (accessed 31 March 2020).
2. United Nations Convention on International Settlement Agreements Resulting from Mediation (New York, 2018) (the "Singapore Convention on Mediation") <https://uncitral.un.org/en/texts/mediation/conventions/international_settlement_agreements> (accessed 1 April 2020).
3. Singapore Convention on Mediation Bill [Bill No. 5/2020).
4. China, India, Germany, Russia and United States of America.
5. The State Courts of Singapore: Code of Ethics and Basic Principles on Court Mediation <https://www.statecourts.gov.sg/cws/Mediation_ADR/Documents/code%20of%20ethics.pdf> (accessed date) ("*Code of Ethics and Basic Principles of Court Mediation*"); State Courts Practice Directions Amendment No. 2 of 2012; State Courts Practice Directions Amendment No. 3 of 2017, Section 35(9)(a).
6. State Courts Practice Directions Amendment No. 2 of 2012.

7. Dorcas Quek Anderson & Kenneth Choo, "Mediation Advocacy for Civil Disputes in the Subordinate Courts: Perspectives from the Bench" (2012) *Singapore Law Gazette* at 14.
8. State Courts Practice Directions Amendment No. 3 of 2017, Section 35(2).
9. Family Justice Act 2014 (No. 27 of 2014).
10. This has been the case since 2014.
11. Supreme Court Practice Directions Amendment No. 1 of 2018, Section 35B(2).
12. Supreme Court Practice Directions, Appendix I: Guidelines for Advocates and Solicitors Advising Clients about ADR.
13. Singapore Mediation Center <https://www.mediation.com.sg/about-us/about-smc/> (accessed 1 April 2020) ("SMC"); Ministry of Law, "Recommendations of the Working Group to develop Singapore into a centre for international commercial mediation" (3 December 2013) <https://www.mlaw.gov.sg/files/news/press-releases/2013/12/FINAL%20ICMWG%20Press%20Release%20-%20Annex%20A.pdf> (accessed 4 April 2020) ("*Press Release*").
14. Singapore Law Watch, "Ch.03 Mediation" <https://www.singaporelawwatch.sg/About-Singapore-Law/Overview/ch-03-mediation#_ftn11> (accessed 1 April 2020) ("*Mediation*").
15. Ibid.
16. Joyce Low & Dorcas Quek Anderson, "Introducing a 'presumption of ADR' for civil matters in the Subordinate Courts" (2012) *Singapore Law Gazette* at 22.
17. Nadja Alexandra, "Ten Trends in International Mediation" (2019) 31 *Singapore Academy of Law Journal* 405.
18. Steven Chong J, "Judicial Reform: Reshaping the Civil Justice System in Singapore", Judicial Conference of the Supreme Courts of G20 (10 October 2019) [unpublished].
19. George Lim & Choo Kin Hua, "Advocacy in Domestic and International Mediations" in Eleanor Wong, Lok Vi Ming SC & The Honourable Justice Vinodh Coomaraswamy, eds., *Modern Advocacy: More Perspectives from Singapore* (Academy Publishing, 2019) at 259.
20. Stephen Covey, *The 7 Habits of Highly Effective People* (Free Press, 1989).
21. Dale Eilerman, "Win/Win Solutions — The Role of Collaboration in Resolving Problems", *Mediate.com* (January 2007) <https://www.mediate.com/articles/eilermanD8.cfm> (accessed 1 April 2020).
22. *Press Release*, see above note 13.
23. Legal Profession (Professional Conduct) Rules 2015, Cap 161 (Rev Ed 2009 Rev).

24. International Mediation Institute, "Competency Criteria for Mediation Advocates and Advisors" <https://www.imimediation.org/orgs/competency-criteria-mediation-advocates-advisors/> (accessed 1 April 2020).
25. European Commission for the Efficiency of Justice (CEPEJ), "Mediation Development Toolkit: Ensuring implementation of the CEPEJ Guidelines on mediation" CEPEJ (2018) 7 Rev.
26. Danny McFadden, "Modern Mediation Defined" in Danny McFadden & George Lim SC, eds., *Mediation in Singapore: A Practical Guide* (Singapore: Sweet & Maxwell, 2015) ("*McFadden*") at 48.
27. *Mediation*, see above note 14.
28. Ibid.
29. *Code of Ethics and Basic Principles of Court Mediation*, see above note 5.
30. *SMC*, see above note 13.
31. *McFadden*, see above note 26.
32. Ibid.
33. *Mediation*, see above note 14.

Chapter 2 Decoding the B.S. (Behavioural Science) in Mediation

1. Deborah Tannen, "What's in a Frame? Surface Evidence for Underlying Expectations" in Roy Freedle, ed., *New Directions in Discourse Processing* (Norwood, NJ: Ablex, 1979).
2. Daniel Kahneman, "Experimental Tests of the Endowment Effect and the Coase Theorem" (1990) 98(6) *The Journal of Political Economy* 1325.
3. Ziv Carmon & Dan Ariely, "Focusing on the Forgone: How Value Can Appear So Different to Buyers and Sellers" (2000) 27(3) *Journal of Consumer Research* 360.
4. Eric J. Johnson, Gerald Häubl & Anat Keinan, "Aspects of Endowment: A Query Theory of Value Construction" (2007) 33(3) *Journal of Experimental Psychology: Learning, Memory, and Cognition* 461.
5. David Gal, "A Psychological Law of Inertia and the Illusion of Loss Aversion" (2006) 1(1) *Judgment and Decision Making* 23.
6. Carey K. Morewedge & Colleen E. Giblin, "Explanations of the Endowment Effect: An Integrative Review" (2015) 19(6) *Trends in Cognitive Sciences* 339.
7. James K. Beggan, "On the Social Nature of Nonsocial Perception: The Mere Ownership Effect" (1992) 62(2) *Journal of Personality and Social Psychology* 229.

8. David A. Hoffman & Richard N. Wolman, "The Psychology of Mediation" (2013) 14 *Cardozo Journal of Conflict Resolution* 759.
9. Roger Fisher & William L. Ury, *Getting to Yes: Negotiating Agreement without Giving In* (Penguin Publishing, 1981).
10. Gregory Klass & Kathryn Zeiler, "Against Endowment Theory: Experimental Economics and Legal Scholarship" (2013) 61 *UCLA Law Review* 2.
11. Ibid at 62: "Does it matter, for example, that subjects do not have a stake in the game? Does it matter that they are students and not practitioners? Does it matter that they have been asked to reach their decision in a relatively short amount of time? Although hypothetical experiments are increasingly common in the legal literature, few legal scholars (and even fewer student editors of law reviews!) have the training necessary to evaluate their methods or the implications of their results with respect to behavior outside the laboratory. When applying the results of such experiments, one should worry that decisions outside the laboratory might be subject to forces that the experimental design has failed to capture, that the outside world is more complex than the one created in the laboratory."
12. Andrea M. Bodtker & Jessica Katz Jameson, "Emotion in Conflict Formation and Its Transformation: Application to Organizational Conflict Management" (2001) 12(3) *International Journal of Conflict Management* 259.
13. Daniel Kahneman, *Thinking, Fast and Slow* (New York: Farrar, Straus and Giroux, 2011).
14. Ibid.
15. Irwin P. Levin, Sandra L. Schneider & Gary J. Gaeth, "All Frames Are Not Created Equal: A Typology and Critical Analysis of Framing Effects" (1998) 76(2) *Organizational Behavior and Human Decision Processes* 149 ("*Levin et al.*").
16. Amos Tversky & Daniel Kahneman, "The Framing of Decisions and the Psychology of Choice" (1981) 211(4481) *Science* 453.
17. Levin *et al.*, see above note 15.
18. Beth E. Meyerowitz & Shelly Chaiken, "The Effect of Message Framing on Breast Self-Examination Attitudes, Intentions, and Behavior" (1987) 52(3) *Journal of Personality and Social Psychology* 500.
19. Joel Lee, "Mediation, Strategic Trust and the Seven Elements" *Kluwer Mediation Blog* (12 December 2019) <http://mediationblog.kluwerarbitration.com/2019/12/12/mediation-strategic-trust-and-the-seven-elements/> (accessed 20 March 2020).

20. Roger Dooley, "How to Use Positive Framing to Persuade and Sell" *Neuromarketing* (2015) <https://www.neurosciencemarketing.com/blog/articles/positive-framing.htm> (accessed 21 March 2020):
"Yale & Duke scientist have conducted experiments on positive and negative framing with primates like chimpanzees and bonobos. They were offered them options for choosing food: either one or two fruits versus a constant number of peanuts. Sometimes the apes were shown one piece of fruit each time they made the selection, but half the time they were given two: (positive framing) In other trials, the apes were initially presented two pieces of fruit, but half the time they got only one: negative framing. Regardless of the framing, the apes ended up with an identical quantity of fruit. Yet they were more likely to choose fruit when they were offered the single fruit with its frequent "bonus" than the double fruit with its frequent "loss."
21. Daniel Kahneman & Amos Tversky, "Prospect Theory: An Analysis of Decision Under Risk" (1979) 47(2) *Econometrica* 263.

Chapter 3 Banking on Mediation: A Critical Analysis of Financial Disputes Mediation in Singapore

1. Shahla Ali, *Consumer Financial Dispute Resolution in a Comparative Context* (Cambridge University Press, 2013) ("*Ali*") at 243.
2. Heng Swee Keat, "Opening Remarks by Mr Heng Swee Keat, Managing Director Monetary Authority of Singapore, at the Launch of the Financial Industry Disputes Resolution Centre (FIDReC)" (31 August 2005) <https://www.mas.gov.sg/news/speeches/2005/opening-remarks-by-mr-heng-swee-keat-for-fidrec> (accessed 5 May 2020).
3. *Ali*, see above note 1 at 190.
4. FIDReC website, "Overview and Background" <https://www.fidrec.com.sg/website/background.html> (accessed 5 May 2020).
5. FIDReC, "Terms of Reference", Rule 5 <https://www.fidrec.com.sg/resources/tor/FIDReC_TOR.pdf> (accessed 5 May 2020) ("*FIDReC Terms of Reference*").
6. "*FIDReC Terms of Reference*", see above note 5 at Rule 4.
7. Ibid.
8. Shahla Ali & Antonio Da Roza, "Alternative Dispute Resolution Design in Financial Markets — Some More Equal Than Others: Hong Kong's Proposed Financial Dispute Resolution Center in the Context of the Experience in the United Kingdom, United States, Australia, and Singapore"

(2012) 21(3) *Pacific Rim Law & Policy Journal* 485 ("*Ali & Da Roza*") at 510.

9. FIDReC, "Annual Report 2018/19" at 5 <https://www.fidrec.com.sg/website/annualreports/FIDReC%20Annual%20Report%202019.pdf> (accessed 5 May 2020) ("*FIDReC Annual Report 2018/19*").
10. FIDReC website, "FIDReC's Jurisdiction" <https://fidrec.com.sg/website/fidrec_jurisdiction.html> (accessed 5 May 2020).
11. "*FIDReC Annual Report 2018/19*" see above note 9 at 6.
12. "*FIDReC Terms of Reference*", see above note 5 at Rule 27.
13. FIDReC website, "Dispute Resolution Process" <https://www.fidrec.com.sg/website/disputerp.html> (accessed 5 May 2020).
14. "*FIDReC Annual Report 2018/19*" see above note 9 at 25.
15. See above note 4.
16. "*FIDReC Terms of Reference*", see above note 5 at Rule 26.
17. See generally FIDReC website, "About the FIDReC-NIMA Scheme" <https://www.fidrec.com.sg/website/aboutfidrec.html> (accessed 5 May 2020).
18. State Courts Practice Directions, Section 37 <https://www.statecourts.gov.sg/cws/Resources/Documents/Master%20PDs%20-%20effective%20PD%206%20of%202019.pdf> (accessed 5 May 2020).
19. Chao Hick Tin J, "Speech by The Honourable Judge of Appeal, Justice Chao Hick Tin, Vice-President of the Court of Appeal, the Guest-of-Honour at the launch of FIDReC-NIMA Scheme at the Subordinate Court" (14 May 2008) <https://www.fidrec.com.sg/website/goh.html> (accessed 5 May 2020).
20. "FIDReC Terms of Reference", see above note 5 at Rule 18A.
21. United Nations Guidelines for Consumer Protection (as adopted by the UN General Assembly in 2015) UNCTAD/DITC/CPLP/MISC/2016/1 <https://unctad.org/en/PublicationsLibrary/ditccplpmisc2016d1_en.pdf> (accessed 5 May 2020) ("*UN Guidelines*").
22. Iris Benöhr, "The United Nations Guidelines for Consumer Protection: Legal Implications and New Frontiers" (2020) 43 *Journal of Consumer Policy* 105 at 113.
23. *UN Guidelines*, see above note 21 at para 37.
24. "*FIDReC Annual Report 2018/19*", see above note 9 at 1.
25. Melanie Lee, "Financial Crisis Politically Awakens Singapore Investors", *Reuters* (7 November 2018) <https://www.reuters.com/article/us-financial-singapore-investors-idUSTRE4A61O320081107> (accessed 5 May 2020).

26. Saw Swee-Hock & John Wong, *Managing Economic Crisis in East Asia* (Institute of Southeast Asian Studies, 2010) at 65.
27. This includes the time taken for all three stages of the FIDReC process: Case Management, Mediation and Adjudication.
28. "*FIDReC Annual Report 2018/19*", see above note 9 at 18.
29. See for example, Singapore Judiciary, "One Judiciary Annual Report 2018" <https://www.supremecourt.gov.sg/docs/default-source/default-document-library/ojar_full-8.pdf> (accessed 5 May 2020).
30. Aloysius Goh, "Chapter 15: Features of a Dispute Suitable for Mediation" in Danny McFadden & George Lim, eds., *Mediation in Singapore: A Practical Guide* (Sweet & Maxwell, 2015) ("*Goh*") at 383.
31. Jacqueline Nolan-Hanley, "Informed Consent in Mediation: A Guiding Principle for Truly Educated Decisionmaking" (1999) 74 *Notre Dame Law Review* 775 at 778.
32. See for example, Joseph Stulberg, "Fairness and Mediation" (1998) 13 *Ohio State Journal on Dispute Resolution* 909 at 911–913.
33. Joan Dworkin & William London, "What is a Fair Agreement?" (1989) 7 *Mediation Quarterly* 3 at 5.
34. Omer Shapira, "Conceptions and Perceptions of Fairness in Mediation" (2012) 54 *South Texas Law Review* 281 at 284.
35. FIDReC website, "FIDReC Training Programme for Mediators of Financial Disputes (FTPM)" <https://www.fidrec.com.sg/website/ftpm_overview.html> (accessed 5 May 2020).
36. FIDReC, "Annual Report 2017/18" at 22 <https://www.fidrec.com.sg/website/annualreports/FIDReC%20Annual%20Report%202019.pdf> (accessed 5 May 2020) ("*FIDReC Annual Report 2017/18*").
37. Ibid. at 21.
38. Nadja Alexander, Joel Lee & Lum Kit-Wye, *Singapore Mediation Handbook* (LexisNexis, 2018) ("*Alexander et al.*") at 366.
39. "*FIDReC Annual Report 2017/18*", see above note 36 at 22.
40. "*FIDReC Terms of Reference*", see above note 5 at Rule 11.
41. Laurence Boulle, *Mediation: Principles, Process, Practice* (LexisNexis, 2011) at 478–479.
42. Larry Haverkamp, "Is FIDReC Fair?" *Singapore Business Review* (21 January 2011) <https://sbr.com.sg/financial-services/commentary/fidrec-fair> (accessed 5 May 2020) ("*Haverkamp*").
43. "*FIDReC Terms of Reference*", see above note 5 at Annex 1.
44. *Ali*, see above note 1 at 146–147.

45. *Haverkamp,* see above note 42.
46. FIDReC website, "Board and Management" <https://www.fidrec.com.sg/website/mgmtboard.html> (accessed 5 May 2020).
47. *Alexander et al.,* see above note 38 at 52.
48. See for example, Charlie Irvine, "Mediation Confidentiality: Limitations and a Proposal" *Kluwer Mediation Blog* (12 September 2012) <http://mediationblog.kluwerarbitration.com/2012/09/12/mediation-confidentiality-limitations-and-a-proposal/> (accessed 5 May 2020).
49. *Goh*, see above note 30 at 381.
50. "FIDReC Annual Report 2018/19" see above note 9 at 6.
51. See above note 43.
52. FDRC website, "Fees — For Cases of Standard Eligible Dispute under Terms of Reference (Jan 2018)" <https://www.fdrc.org.hk/en/html/resolvingdisputes/resolvingdisputes_scheduleoffees.php> (accessed 5 May 2020).
53. Nelson Goh, "Navigating the Minefield of Equity Release Products for Elders" (2014) 26 *Singapore Academy of Law Journal* 461 at 496.
54. ASEAN 5 refers to the five largest economies in the Association of Southeast Asian Nations, namely Malaysia, Singapore, Thailand, Indonesia and the Philippines.
55. Vivien Chen, Andrew Goodwin & Ian Ramsay, "An ASEAN Framework for Cross-Border Cooperation in Financial Consumer Dispute Resolution" (2017) 12 *Asian Journal of Comparative Law* 167 at 191.
56. Ibid.
57. "*FIDReC Annual Report 2017/18*", see above note 36 at 34–41.
58. Monetary Authority of Singapore (Dispute Resolution Schemes) Regulations 2007 (GN S 436/2007).
59. *Ali*, see above note 1 at 149.
60. "*FIDReC Annual Report 2017/18*", see above note 36 at 13.
61. Ibid.
62. See for example, MoneySense, "Resolving a Dispute with a Financial Institution" (5 November 2018) <https://www.moneysense.gov.sg/articles/2018/11/resolving-a-dispute-with-a-financial-institution> (accessed 5 May 2020).
63. FIDReC website, "Contact Us" <https://www.fidrec.com.sg/website/contactus.html> (accessed 5 May 2020).
64. *Ali*, see above note 1 at 150.
65. "*FIDReC Annual Report 2018/19*" see above note 9 at 3.
66. *Ali*, see above note 1 at 210.
67. *Ali*, see above note 1 at 211.
68. *Alexander et al.*, see above note 38 at 121.

69. *Ali & Da Roza*, see above note 8 at 515.
70. Nadja Alexander, "The Mediation Meta-Model: Understanding Practice" 26(1) *Conflict Resolution Quarterly* 97 at 107–108.
71. Alexander *et al.*, see above note 38 at 118.
72. *Ali*, see above note 1 at 210.
73. Mediation Act (No. 1 of 2017), Section 9(2)(d).
74. "*FIDReC Terms of Reference*", see above note 5 at Rule 6.
75. Monetary Authority of Singapore, "Response to Feedback Received — Consultation on the Financial Industry Disputes Resolution Centre (FIDReC)" <https://www.mas.gov.sg/-/media/MAS/resource/publications/consult_papers/2004/Responses-to-Feedback-Received-FIDReC.pdf> (accessed 5 May 2020).
76. *Ali*, see above note 1 at 193.
77. FIDReC, "Annual Report 2012/13" at 3 <https://www.fidrec.com.sg/website/annualreports/FIDReC%20AR%202012-2013.pdf> (accessed 5 May 2020).
78. Chief Justice of Hong Kong Andrew Li, "Speech at the Ceremonial Opening of the Legal Year 2010" (11 January 2010) <https://www.info.gov.hk/gia/general/201001/11/P201001110174.htm> (accessed 5 May 2020).

Chapter 4 Why Not Have the Best of Both Worlds? A Framework to Interlink Collaborative Law and Mediation to Resolve Personal Disputes

1. Anne Barlow, Rosemary Hunter, Janet Smithson & Jan Ewing, *Mapping Paths to Family Justice: Resolving Family Disputes in Neoliberal Times* (London: Palgrave Macmillan, 2017).
2. Josiane Fahed-Sreih, *Conflict in Family Businesses: Conflict, Models, and Practices* (Palgrave Macmillan, 2018).
3. Ilan G. Gewurz, "(Re)designing Mediation to Address the Nuances of Power Imbalance" (2001) 19(2) *Conflict Resolution Quarterly* 135.
4. Diana S. Marinova, "Neutrality in mediation hearings: Managing the mediation process without bias" (Doctoral Dissertation), (2008) Georgetown University.
5. Martha E. Simmons, "Collaborative Law at 25: A Canadian Study of a Global Phenomenon" (2016) 49(2) *University of British Columbia Law Review* 669 at 698.
6. Bobette Wolski, "Collaborative Law: An (Un)ethical Process for Lawyers?" (2017) 20(2) *Legal Ethics* 224.

7. David A Hoffman, "Exploring the Boundaries and Terrain of ADR Practice: Mediation, Arbitration, and Collaborative Law" (2007–08) 14 *Dispute Resolution Magazine* 4.
8. Michael A. Zeytoonian, "One Key Difference Between Mediation and Collaborative Law is Often Overlooked", *Mediate.com* (February 2012) <https://www.mediate.com/articles/ZeytoonianMbl20120228.cfm> (accessed 2 March 2020).
9. Stephen B. Goldberg, Jeanne M. Brett, Beatrice Blohorn-Brenneur & Nancy H. Rogers, *How Mediation Works: Theory, Research, and Practice* (Bingley, UK: Emerald Publishing, 2017).
10. Shirley Shipman, Ben Waters, William Wood & Henry Brown, *Brown & Marriott's ADR Principles and Practice* (London: Sweet & Maxwell/ Thomson Reuters, 4th Edition, 2018).
11. Kelly Chandler-Olcott & Kathleen A. Hinchman, "Mediation" (2018) 62(1) Journal of Adolescent & Adult Literacy 5.
12. Marian Roberts, *Mediation in Family Disputes: Principles of Practice* (Routledge, 4th Edition, 2014).
13. See above note 11.
14. Ibid.
15. See above note 1.
16. Jacqueline M. Nolan-Haley, "Informed Consent in Mediation: A Guiding Principle for Truly Educated Decision Making" (1999) 74 *Notre Dame Law Review* 775.
17. Jim Hilbert, "Collaborative Lawyering: A Process for Interest-based Negotiation" (2010) 38(4) *Hofstra Law Review* 1083.
18. See above note 7.
19. see above note 9.
20. John M. Lande, "Possibilities for Collaborative Law: Ethics and Practice of Lawyer Disqualification and Process Control in a New Model of Lawyering" (2003) 64(5) *Ohio State Law Journal* 1315.
21. See above note 9.
22. Gregg Herman, "ADR and Family Law" (2008) 14(3–4) *Dispute Resolution Magazine* 37.
23. Ibid.
24. Mavis Maclea & Bregje Dijksterhuis, *Digital Family Justice: From Alternative Dispute Resolution to Online Dispute Resolution?* (New York: Hart Publishing, 2019).
25. Liz Trinder, Joanne Kellet & Louise Swift, "The Relationship Between Contact and Child Adjustment in High Conflict Cases after Divorce or Separation" (2008) 13(4) *Child and Adolescent Mental Health* 181.

26. Noel Semple, "Mandatory Family Mediation and the Settlement Mission: A Feminist Critique" (2012) 24(1) *Canadian Journal of Women and the Law* 207.
27. Judy Gutman, "Litigation as a Measure of Last Resort: Opportunities and Challenges for Legal Practitioners with the Rise of ADR" (2011) 14(1) *Legal Ethics* 1.
28. Elizabeth F. Beyer, "A Pragmatic Look at Mediation and Collaborative Law as Alternatives to Family Law" (2008) 40(1) *St. Mary's Law Journal* 303.
29. Gary L. Voegele, Ronald D. Ousky & Linda K. Wray, "Collaborative Law: A Useful Tool for the Family Law Practitioner to Promote Better Outcomes" (2007) 33(3) *William Mitchell Law Review* 971.
30. John Lande & Forrest Steven Mosten, "Before You Take a Collaborative Law Case: What the Ethical Rules Say About Conflicts of Interest, Client Screening, and Informed Consent" (2010) 33(2) *Family Advocate* 31.
31. Penny Brooker, *Mediation law: Journey through Institutionalism to Juridification* (Routledge, 2013).
32. Elizabeth A. Hoffmann, "Compromise, Confrontation, and Coercion: Formal and Informal Dispute Resolution in Cooperative and Hierarchical Worksites" (Doctoral Dissertation), (2001) University of Wisconsin-Madison.
33. Noble T. Foster & Selden Prentice, "The Promise of Confidentiality in Mediation: Practitioners' Perceptions" (2009) (1) *Journal of Dispute Resolution* 163.
34. James Pirrie, "Collaborative Divorce" (2006) 156(7227) *New Law Journal* 898.
35. Pauline H. Tesler, "Collaborative Family Law", (2004) 4(3) *Pepperdine Dispute Resolution Law Journal* 317.
36. See above note 34.
37. Ibid.
38. See above note 2.
39. See above note 29.
40. See above note 2.
41. See above note 7.

Chapter 5 The Functions of Artificial Intelligence in Mediation

1. Nick Hilborne, "Robot mediator settles first ever court case", *LegalFutures UK* (19 February 2019).
2. Davide Carneiro, Paulo Novais & José Neves, *Conflict Resolution and its Context: From the Analysis of Behavioural Patterns to Efficient Decision-Making* (Springer, 2014) ("*Carneiro et al.*") at 62.

3. John R. Searle, "Minds, brains and programs" (1980) 3(3) *Behavioral and Brain Sciences* 41.
4. Alan Turing, "Computing machinery and intelligence" (1950) 59 *Mind* 433.
5. Kate Beioley, "Robots and AI threaten to mediate disputes better than lawyers", *Financial Times* (14 August 2019).
6. Daniel J. Olsher, "New Artificial Intelligence Tools for Deep Conflict Resolution and Humanitarian Response" (2015) 107 *Procedia Engineering* 282.
7. Ibid.
8. *Carneiro et al.,* see above note 2 at 70.
9. Davide Carneiro, Paulo Novais & José Neves, "Using Genetic Algorithms to Create Solutions for Conflict Resolution", (2013) 109 *Neurocomputing* 16.
10. John Zeleznikow & Andrew Stranieri, 1995. "The Split-up System: Integrating Neural Networks and Rule-based Reasoning in the Legal Domain". In *Proceedings of the 5th international conference on Artificial Intelligence and law* (1995) 185.
11. *Carneiro et al.,* see above note 2 at 65.
12. Janet Kolodner & Robert L. Simpson, "The MEDIATOR: Analysis of an Early Case-based Problem Solver" (1989) 13(4) *Cognitive Science* 507.
13. Ibid.
14. Katia P. Sycara, "Machine Learning for Intelligent Support of Conflict Resolution" (1993) 10(2) *Decision Support Systems* 121.
15. *Carneiro et al.*, see above note 2 at 78.
16. David Allen Larson, "Artificial Intelligence: Robots, Avatars, and the Demise of the Human Mediator" (2010) 25(1) *Ohio State Journal on Dispute Resolution* 105.
17. Ibid.
18. *Carneiro et al.*, see above note 2 at 88.

Chapter 6 Confidentiality in the Singapore Mediation Scene: Is It Sufficient or Can More Be Done?

1. Dorcas Quek Anderson, "Piercing the Veil of Confidentiality in Mediation to Ensure Good Faith Participation: An Untenable Position?" (2019) 31 *Singapore Academy of Law Journal* 713 ("*Anderson*") at 716.
2. Bruce Pardy & Charles Pou, "Confidentiality" in Ellen Waldman, ed., *Mediation Ethics: Cases and Commentaries* (San Francisco: Jossey-Bass, 2011) at 55.

3. Nadja Alexander, Joel Lee & Lum Kit-Wye, *Singapore Mediation Handbook* (Singapore: LexisNexis, 2019) ("*Alexander et al.*") at 446–447.
4. Ibid at 439.
5. Laurence Boulle and Teh Hwee Hwee, *Mediation: Principles, Process, Practice* (Singapore: Butterworths Asia, 2000) ("*Boulle and Teh*") at 329.
6. UNCITRAL Model Law on International Commercial Mediation and International Settlement Agreements Resulting from Mediation, 2018 (amending the UNCITRAL Model Law on International Commercial Conciliation, 2002).
7. *Boulle and Teh*, see above note 5 at 329.
8. Ibid.
9. Jo-Anne Bigham, "Confidentiality and Without Prejudice: Illusory or Real?" (2006] 1 Asian Journal on Mediation 13 ("*Bigham*") at 15.
10. Raymond Hai Ming Leung, *Asia Mediation Handbook* (Hong Kong: Sweet & Maxwell, 2015) at 438.
11. *Boulle and Teh*, see above note 5 at 329.
12. *Bigham*, see above note 9.
13. Singapore Law Watch, "Ch.03 Mediation" <https://www.singaporelaw-watch.sg/About-Singapore-Law/Overview/ch-03-mediation> (accessed 4 April 2020).
14. Ibid.
15. X Pte Ltd and another v CDE [1992] 2 SLR(R) 575 at [27].
16. David Spencer & Michael Brogan, *Mediation Law and Practice* (Melbourne: Cambridge University Press, 2007) at 313.
17. Nadene Law Qin Ning, "The Case for Confidentiality: Singapore's Mediation Act" in Joel Lee & Marcus Lim, eds., Contemporary Issues in Mediation Volume 4 (Singapore: World Scientific, 2019) ("*Law*") at 61.
18. Ibid at 62.
19. *Boulle and Teh*, see above note 5 at 340.
20. Christopher W Moore, *Mediation Process: Practical Strategies for Resolving Conflict* (San Francisco: Joey-Bass Publishers, 2nd edition,1996) at 156.
21. John Michael Richardson, "How Confidential Is Mediation Confidentiality?" in Arthur W. Rovine, ed., *Contemporary Issues in International Arbitration and Mediation: The Fordham Papers* (Brill, 2018) at 273.
22. Quek Kheng Leong Nicky and another v Teo Beng Ngoh and others and another appeal [2009] 4 SLR(R) 181 at [22].
23. *Anderson*, see above 1 at 716.
24. Evidence Act (Cap 97) Rev Ed 1997.

25. Mariwu Industrial Co (S) Pte Ltd v Dextra Asia Co Ltd [2006] 4 SLR(R) 807 at [28].
26. Ng Chee Weng v Lim Jit Ming Bryan [2010] SGHC 35 at [8]–[11].
27. Unilever Plc v The Procter & Gamble Co [2000] 1 WLR 2436 at 2444–2445.
28. Ng Chee Weng v Lim Jit Ming Bryan [2012] 1 SLR 457 at [95]–[97]; Quek Kheng Leong Nicky and another v Teo Beng Ngoh and others and another appeal [2009] 4 SLR(R) 181 ("*Quek v Teo*") at [23]–[24].
29. *Quek v Teo*, see above note 27 at [24].
30. *Anderson*, see above note 1 at 720–721.
31. *Boulle and Teh*, see above note 5 at 344.
32. *Anderson*, see above note 1, 715.
33. Ibid.
34. Mediation Act 2017 (No. 1 of 2017) ("*Mediation Act*").
35. *Singapore Parliamentary Debates: Official Report*, Vol 94 (10 January 2017) (Senior Minister of State for Law: Indranee Rajah S.C.) ("*Parliamentary Debates*").
36. Joel Lee, "Singapore Developments — The Mediation Act 2016" *Kluwer Mediation Blog* (March 12, 2017).
37. *Alexander et al.,* see above note 3 at 440.
38. *Parliamentary Debates,* see above note 35.
39. Ibid.
40. *Alexander et al.*, see above note 3 at 467.
41. *Anderson*, see above note 1 at 723.
42. *Law*, see above note 17 at 64.
43. *Parliamentary Debates*, see above note 35.
44. Community Mediation Centres Act, Cap 49A (Rev Ed 1998).
45. *Law*, see above note 17 at 63.
46. Ibid.
47. Uniform Mediation Act (2003), USA.
48. *Anderson*, see above note 1 at 724.
49. Dorcas Quek Anderson, "Litigating Over Mediation — How Should the Courts Enforce Mediated Settlement Agreements?" (2015) 1 *Singapore Journal of Legal Studies* 105 ("*Quek*") at 133.
50. Ellen E Deason, "Enforcing Mediated Settlement Agreements: Contract Law Collides with Confidentiality" (April 2001) 35 *UC Davis Law Review* 33 at 68.
51. Ibid.

52. *Parliamentary Debates*, see above note 35.
53. AB v CD Limited [2013] EWHC 1376.
54. Surindar Singh s/o Jaswant Singh v Sita Jaswant Kaur [2014] 3 SLR 1284.
55. *Quek*, see above note 49 at 127.
56. Ibid.

Chapter 7 Online Mediation: The Future that Arrived Much Sooner Than We Thought

1. Haitham Haloush & Bashar Malkawi, "Internet Characteristics and Online Alternative Dispute Resolution" (2008) 13 *Harvard Negotiation Law Review* 327 ("*Haloush & Malkawi*") at 332.
2. Paul Breaux, "Online Dispute Resolution: A Modern Alternative Dispute Resolution Approach" (2015) 32(5) *The Computer & Internet Lawyer* 1 ("*Breaux*"); Christopher Honeyman and Andrea Schneider, eds., *The Negotiator's Desk Reference, Volume 1* (DRI Press, 2017) ("*Honeyman & Schneider*") at 190.
3. See Kee Oon J, Presiding Judge of the State Courts (then), "Shaping Tomorrow's Justice", keynote address at the State Courts Workplan 2018 (9 March 2018) https://www.statecourts.gov.sg/cws/Resources/Documents/StateCourtsWorkplan%202018_Keynote_Address.pdf (accessed 30 May 2020); State Courts, "State Courts Launch Online Filing for Neighbour Disputes", media release on the second phase of the State Courts' Community Justice and Tribunals System (5 February 2018) https://www.statecourts.gov.sg/cws/NewsAndEvents/Documents/MediaRelease_CJTS%20Phase2_5Feb2018V140218.pdf (accessed 30 May 2020) ("*State Courts*"); *Honeyman & Schneider*, see above note 2 at 190.
4. Ethan Katsh & Janet Rifkin, *Online Dispute Resolution: Resolving Conflicts in Cyberspace* (Wiley, 2001); Nadja Alexander, "Ten Trends in International Mediation" (2019) 31 *Singapore Academy of Law Journal* 405 ("*Alexander*") at 436.
5. Daniel Rainey, "Third-Party Ethics in the Age of the Fourth Party" (2014) 1(1) *International Journal of Online Dispute Resolution* 37 at 37–38.
6. See generally, Ethan Katsh, Daniel Rainey, Mohamed S. Abdel & Richard Susskind, eds., *Online Dispute Resolution: Theory and Practice* (Eleven International Publishing, 2012) ("*Katsh et al.*") at 369–398; *Breaux*, see above note 2; *Honeyman & Schneider*, see above note 2.

7. *Honeyman & Schneider*, see above note 2 at 187.
8. Lydia Lam, "'Surreal' and 'seamless': 115 lawyers called to the Bar via video conference in a first for Singapore", *Channel News Asia* (13 May 2020) <https://www.channelnewsasia.com/news/singapore/lawyers-called-to-the-bar-video-conference-first-in-singapore-12728678> (accessed 30 May 2020).
9. See Sandhya Swaminathan and Kartiyeka Singh, "Mediating Amidst a Crisis: Is Online Mediation a Solution for India?" *Mediate.com* (May 2020) <https://www.mediate.com/articles/swaminathan-online-india.cfm> (accessed 30 May 2020); Jacques Joubert, "Courts Mediating Online with Zoom" *Mediate.com* (April 2020) <https://www.mediate.com/articles/joubert-zoom.cfm> (accessed 30 May 2020); Morenike Obi-Farinde, "ODR in Africa: The Emergent Face of Dispute Resolution Post COVID 19", *Mediate.com* (April 2020) <https://www.mediate.com/articles/obi-odr-africa.cfm>> (accessed 30 May 2020).
10. Christopher Moore, *The Mediation Process: Practical Strategies for Resolving Conflict* (John Wiley & Sons, 4th Edition, 2014) at 19–28.
11. Harvard Law School Program on Negotiation, "Technology makes online mediation and professional dispute resolution more accessible" *Harvard Law School Program on Negotiation Daily Blog* (27 January 2020) <https://www.pon.harvard.edu/daily/mediation/dispute-resolution-using-online-mediation/> (accessed 30 May 2020) ("*Harvard Law School Program on Negotiation*"; Christopher Honeyman, James Coben & Giuseppe De Palo, eds., *Rethinking Negotiation Teaching: Innovations for Context and Culture* (CreateSpace Independent Publishing Platform, 2009) ("*Honeyman et al.*") at 89–114.
12. *Harvard Law School Program on Negotiation*, see above note 11.
13. Harvard Law School Program on Negotiation, "Types of Mediation: Choose the Type Best Suited to Your Conflict" *Harvard Law School Program on Negotiation Daily Blog* (7 May 2020) <https://www.pon.harvard.edu/daily/mediation/types-mediation-choose-type-best-suited-conflict/> (accessed 30 May 2020); see also Paula Young, "Online Mediation: Its Uses and Limitations", *Mediate.com* <https://www.mediate.com/articles/young4.cfm> (accessed 30 May 2020).
14. Nadja Alexander, "Mobile mediation: How technology is driving the globalization of ADR" (2006) 27(2) *Hamline Journal of Public Law and Policy* 243 ("*Alexander*"); Jeremy Barnett and Philip Treleaven, "Algorithmic Dispute Resolution — The Automation of Professional Dispute Resolution Using AI and Blockchain Technologies" (2018) 61(3) *The Computer Journal* 399; Tim

Constable and Sonia Vilar, "Blind bidding — the next logical step in remote mediation", *Dentons* (7 May 2020) <https://www.dentons.com/en/insights/articles/2020/may/7/blind-bidding-the-next-logical-step-in-remote-mediation> (accessed 30 May 2020).

15. *Alexander*, see above note 14; *Honeyman & Schneider*, see above note 2 at 190; *State Courts*, see above note 3.
16. *Katsh et al.*, see above note 6 at 367–368.
17. Ibid.
18. Jordan Goldberg, "Online Alternative Dispute Resolution and Why Law Schools Should Prepare Future Lawyers for the Online Forum" (2014) 14(1) *Pepperdine Dispute Resolution Law Journal* 1 ("*Goldberg*") at 13–14.
19. Joseph Goodman, "The Advantages and Disadvantages of Online Dispute Resolution: An Assessment of Cyber-Mediation Web Sites" (2006) 9(11) *Journal of Internet Law* 1 ("*Goodman*") at 13; Mimoza Sadushi, "The Theory and Practice of Dispute Resolution in the Digital Age" (2017) 5(7) *Global Journal of Politics and Law Research* 57 ("*Sadushi*") at 64–65.
20. *Haloush & Malkawi*, see above note 1 at 339; Sadushi, see above note 19; *Katsh et al.*, see above note 6 at 365.
21. William Ury, *Getting Past No* (Batam Books, Rev Ed, 1993) at 37.
22. Richard Daft and Robert Lengel, "Information Richness. A New Approach to Managerial Behavior and Organization Design" (1984) 6 *Research in Organisational Behaviour* 191; *Honeyman et al.*, see above note 11 at 91–92; *Goldberg*, see above note 18 at 16–17.
23. *Honeyman et al.*, see above note 11.
24. *Haloush & Malkawi*, see above note 1 at 338.
25. Susan Nauss Exon & Soomi Lee, "Building Trust Online: The Realities of Telepresence for Mediators Engaged in Online Dispute Resolution" (2019) 49 *Stetson Law Review* 109 ("*Exon & Lee*") at 128; Kevin Rockmann & Gregory Northcraft, "To be or not to be trusted: The influence of media richness on defection and deception" (2008) 107 *Organizational Behavior and Human Decision Processes* 106 ("*Rockmann & Northcraft*") at 108.
26. William D'Zurilla, "Alternative Dispute Resolution" (1997) 45 *Los Angeles Business Journal* 352; *Goodman*, see above note 19 at 13; *Sadushi*, see above note 19 at 62–63.
27. *Exon & Lee*, see above note 25 at 120.
28. Noam Ebner & Jeff Thompson, "Face Value: Non-Verbal Communication and Trust Development in Online Video-Based Mediation" (2014) 1 *International Journal of Online Dispute Resolution* 103 ("*Ebner & Thompson*") at 106.

29. See David Nguyen & John Canny, "MultiView: Improving Trust in Group Video Conferencing Through Spatial Faithfulness" (2007) *Proceedings of the SIGCHI Conference on Human Factors in Computing Systems* 1465 ("*Nguyen & Canny*"); *Goldberg*, see above note 18; *Rockmann and Northcraft*, see above note 25; cf. *Exon & Lee*, see above note 25; Nathan Bos, Darren Gergle, Judith S. Olson & Gary M. Olson, "Being There Versus Seeing There: Trust via Video" (2001) *Conference on Human Factors in Computing Systems: Extended Abstracts on Human Factors in Computing Systems* 291.
30. *Ebner & Thompson*, see above note 28.
31. Petr Slovák, "Effect of Videoconferencing Environments on Perception of Communication" (2007) 1(1) *Cyberpsychology: Journal of Psychosocial Research on Cyberspace* Article 8.
32. *Nguyen & Canny*, see above note 29.
33. See for example, Suzanne Segal, "Effective Virtual Mediation During the Coronavirus Crisis", *Bloomberg Law* (9 April 2020) <https://news.bloomberglaw.com/us-law-week/insight-effective-virtual-mediation-during-the-coronavirus-crisis> (accessed 30 May 2020); Keith Ferrazzi, "How to Run a Great Virtual Meeting", *Havard Business Review* (27 March 2015) <https://hbr.org/2015/03/how-to-run-a-great-virtual-meeting> (accessed 30 May 2020).
34. Kumi Ishii, Mary Lyons & Sabrina Carr, "Revisiting media richness theory for today and future" (2019) 1 *Human Behaviour and Emerging Technology* 124 at 128.
35. Siti Hamin Stapa & Azianura Hani Shaari, "Understanding Online Communicative Language Features in Social Networking Environment" (2012) 12(3) *Journal of Language Studies* 817 at 820; see also Oren Soffer, "Liquid language? On the personalization of discourse in the digital era" (2012) 14(7) *New Media & Society* 1092.
36. See for example, Danielle N. Gunraj, April M. Drumm-Hewitt, Erica M. Dashow, Sri Sidhi N. Upadhyay & Celia M. Klin, "Texting Insincerely: The Role of the Period in Text Messaging" (2016) 55 *Computers in Human Behaviour* 1067; Kenneth J. Houghton, Sri Siddhi N. Upadhyay & Celia M. Klin, "Punctuation in text messages may convey abruptness. Period" (2018) 80 *Computers in Human Behaviour* 112.
37. See generally, Dominic Thompson & Ruth Filik, "Sarcasm in Written Communication: Emoticons are Efficient Markers of Intention" (2016) 21 *Journal of Computer-Mediated Communication* 105; Bai Qiyu, Dan Qi, Mu Zhe & Yang Maokun, "A Systematic Review of Emoji: Current Research and

Future Perspectives" (2019) 10 *Frontiers in Psychology Article* 2221; Monica Riordan, "Emojis as Tools for Emotion Work: Communicating Affect in Text Messages" (2017) 36(5) *Journal of Language and Social Psychology* 549.

38. Elza Venter, "Bridging the Communication Gap between Generation Y and the Baby Boomer Generation" (2016) 22(4) *International Journal of Adolescence and Youth* 497 ("*Venter*") at 502–503; Stephen Kuyath & Susan Winter, "Distance Education Communications: The Social Presence and Media Richness of Instant Messaging" (2006) 10(4) *Journal of Asynchronous Learning Networks* 67 at 72.
39. *Venter*, see above note 38 at 504–505.
40. Paul Grice, *Studies in the Way of Words* (Harvard University Press, 1991) at 2–40.
41. Ibid.
42. *Alexander*, see above note 4 at 420–424.
43. Rafal Morek, "*Nihil Silentio Utilius*: Confidentiality in Mediation and Its Legal Safeguards in the EU Member States" (2013) 14 *ERA Forum* 421 at 422.
44. Norman Solovay & Cynthia Reed, *The Internet and Dispute Resolution: Untangling the Web* (Law Journal Press, 2003) at 8–21.
45. See for example, Farm Assist Ltd v Secretary of State for the Environment, Food and Rural Affairs [2009] All ER (D) 228 (Jun); I-Admin (Singapore) Pte Ltd v Hong Ying Ting [2020] SGCA 32.
46. Catharine Titi & Katia Fach Gomez, eds., *Mediation in International Commercial and Investment Disputes* (Oxford University Press, 2019) at 11.
47. See for example Kari Paul, "'Zoom is malware': why experts worry about the video conferencing platform", *The Guardian* (2 April 2020) <https://www.theguardian.com/technology/2020/apr/02/zoom-technology-security-coronavirus-video-conferencing> (accessed 30 May 2020); Hariz Baharudin, "Coronavirus: No more Zoom for home-based learning after hackers show obscene photos to Singapore students", *The Straits Times* (9 April 2020) <https://www.straitstimes.com/singapore/hackers-hijack-home-based-lessons-on-zoom-to-allegedly-show-obscene-photos-to-children> (accessed 30 May 2020).
48. See for example Eric Yuan, A Message to Our Users", *Zoom* (3 April 2020) <https://blog.zoom.us/response-to-research-from-university-of-torontos-citizen-lab/> (accessed 15 June 2021); Paul Wagenseil, "Zoom security issues: Here's everything that's gone wrong (so far)", *Tom's Guide* (5 June 2021) <https://www.tomsguide.com/news/zoom-security-privacy-woes> (accessed 15 June 2021).

Chapter 8 Exploring What Mediation Looks Like in the Religious Spheres of Islam and Christianity

1. Leonard L. Riskin, "Understanding Mediators' Orientations, Strategies and Techniques: A Grid for the Perplexed" (1996) 1 *Harvard Negotiation Law Review* 7 at 13.
2. Christopher To, "Facilitative Versus Evaluative Mediation" (2018) 20(2) *Asian Dispute Review* 81 at 84–85.
3. Ibid. at 83.
4. Carole J. Brown, "Facilitative Mediation: The Classic Approach Retains Its Appeal" (2004) 4(2) *Pepperdine Dispute Resolution Law Journal* 283.
5. Kenneth Wayne Thomas & Ralph H. Kimann, *Thomas-Kilmann Conflict Mode Instrument* (Mountain View, CA: CPP, 1974).
6. *The Holy Bible: English Standard Version* (HarperCollins, 2008) ("*The Bible*") at 1 Corinthians 6:7
7. Ibid at Matthew 18:15–17. "If your brother sins against you, go and tell him his fault, between you and him alone. If he listens to you, you have gained your brother. But if he does not listen, take one or two others along with you, that every charge may be established by the evidence of two or three witnesses. If he refuses to listen to them, tell it to the church. And if he refuses to listen even to the church, let him be to you as a Gentile and a tax collector."
8. *The Bible*, see above note 6 at John 17:20–21. "I do not ask for these only, but also for those who will believe in me through their word, that they may all be one, just as you, Father, are in me, and I in you, that they also may be in us, so that the world may believe that you have sent me."
9. John Bevere, *The Bait of Satan: Living Free from the Deadly Trap of Offense* (Charisma Media, 2014).
10. *The Bible*, see above note 6 at Philippians 2:3–4. "Do nothing out of selfish ambition or vain conceit. Rather, in humility value others above yourselves, not looking to your own interests but each of you to the interests of the others."
11. *The Bible*, see above note 6 at Matthew 22:39. "And a second is like it: You shall love your neighbour as yourself".
12. *The Bible*, see above note 6 at Colossians 3:13. "bearing with one another and, if one has a complaint against another, forgiving each other; as the Lord has forgiven you, so you also must forgive."

13. Mohammed Abu-Nimer & David Augsburger, eds., *Peace-Building by, between, and beyond Muslims and Evangelical Christians* (Lexington Books, 2009).
14. Arif A Jamal, "ADR and Islamic law: The Cases of the UK and Singapore", NUS Law Working Paper No. 2015/004.
15. Khalid Iqbal, Islamic Mediation <http://www.rahmaa.org/domesticviolence/islamic-mediation/> (accessed 28 March 2020).
16. *The Qur'an*. Translated by Sahih International ("*The Quran*") at 4:35.
17. H.L. Hafdane, *Mediation in Modern Morocco: Realities and Challenges After the National Reconciliation of 2001* (Search for Common Ground Series: Merging Methods of Alternative Dispute Resolution and Mediation in Morocco, 2013).
18. *The Quran*, see above note 16 at 4:59.
19. *The Quran*, see above note 16 at 49:9.
20. *The Quran*, see above note 16 at 5:9 and 4:135.
21. *The Quran*, see above note 16 at 4:65.
22. *The Quran*, see above note 16 at 4:35.
23. *The Quran*, see above note 16 at 8:1.
24. Abdur Rahman Doi, *Shariah: Islamic Law* (Ta-Ha Publishers, 2008) at 358–359.
25. N.J. Coulson, *A History of Islamic Law* (Aldine Transaction, 2011).

Chapter 9 Is Mediation an Appropriate Forum for Dispute Resolution in the Context of Domestic Violence?

1. Nadja Alexander, "Mediation in Practice: Common Law and Civil Law Perspectives Compared" (2001) 6 *International Trade and Business Law Annual* 1 at 4.
2. Joyce Fong, "The Singapore Convention on Mediation — the beginning of a new era?" Reed Smith Client Alerts (7 August 2019).
3. Rene L. Rimelspach, "Mediating Family Disputes in a World with Domestic Violence: How To Devise a Safe and Effective Court-Connected Mediation Program" (2001) 17(1) *Ohio State Journal on Dispute Resolution* 95 ("*Rimelspach*").
4. Joan B. Kelly "Power Imbalance in Divorce and Interpersonal Mediation: Assessment and Intervention" (1995) 13(2) *Mediation Quarterly* 85.
5. Rachel M Field, "Mediation and the Art of Power (Im)Balancing" (1996) 12 *Queensland University of Technology Law Journal* 264 ("*Field*").
6. *Field*, see above note 5 at 266.

7. Lisa G. Lerman, "Mediation of Wife Abuse Cases: The Adverse Impact of Informal Dispute Resolution on Women" (1984) 7 *Harvard Women's Law Journal* 57 ("*Lerman*").
8. Ibid. at 102–103.
9. Margaret B. Drew, "Collaboration and Coercion: Domestic Violence Meets Collaborative Law" (2012) 1 *Irish Law Journal* 27.
10. Ibid. at 41.
11. Susan Landrum, "The Ongoing Debate about Mediation in the Context of Domestic Violence: A Call for Empirical Studies of Mediation Effectiveness" (2011) 12 *Cardozo Journal of Conflict Resolution* 425 ("*Landrum*").
12. Ibid. at 436.
13. Amrita Narine, "Power Imbalances in Mediation" (2017) *Harvard Negotiation Law Review* ("*Narine*").
14. Richard M. Tolman, Ph.D., Tolman Screening Model.
15. *Narine*, see above note 13 at 12.
16. Ibid. at 13.
17. *Landrum*, see above note 11 at 440.
18. *Lerman*, see above note 7 at 93.
19. *Field*, see above note 5 at 269.
20. *Landrum*, see above note 11 at 445.
21. *Rimelspach*, see above note 3 at 99.
22. Ali Khaled Qtaishat, "Power Imbalances in Mediation" (2018) 14(2) *Asian Social Science* 75.
23. *Landrum*, see above note 11 at 446.
24. Sandra Zaher, "The Feminization of Family Mediation" (1998) 53(2) Dispute Resolution Journal 36 at 41.
25. *Rimelspach*, see above note 3 at 102.
26. Desmond Ellis, Family Mediation Pilot Project Final Report, Ministry of the Attorney General, Toronto, Ontario, July 1994.

Chapter 10 Lessons from Transformative Mediation and How It Can Benefit Singapore's Mediation Landscape

1. United Nations Convention on International Settlement Agreements Resulting from Mediation (New York, 2018).
2. For instance, Court Dispute Resolution has been described as directive or evaluative, as Lee and Teh note.
3. Joel Lee & Teh Hwee Hwee, *An Asian Perspective on Mediation* (Academy Publishing, 2009) ("*Lee & Teh*") at 13.

4. Roger Fisher & William L. Ury, *Getting to Yes: Negotiating Agreement without Giving In* (Penguin Publishing, 1981).
5. Kenny Yang, "Towards Cross-Cultural Fluency in Mediation Standards" (2017) 36(1) *University of Tasmania Law Review* 69 ("*Yang*") at 73.
6. Robert A. Baruch Bush & Joseph P. Folger, *The Promise of Mediation: The Transformative Approach to Conflict* (Jossey-Bass, 2004) ("*Bush & Folger*").
7. Rich L. Skalstad, "Transformative Mediation Twenty Years Later: An Invitation to Discuss Post-Traumatic Stress Disorder and Legal Ethics" (2016) 1(1) *Concordia Law Review* 1 ("*Skalstad*") at 4.
8. Robert Condlin, "The Curious Case of Transformative Dispute Resolution: An Unfortuante Marriage of Intransigence, Exclusivity, and Hype" (2013) (14)(3) *Cardozo Journal of Conflict Resolution* 621; Michael Williams, "Can't I get No Satisfaction? Thoughts on the Promise of Mediation" (1997) 15(2) *Mediation Quarterly* 143.
9. Tina Nabatchi, Lisa Blomgren Bingham & Yuseok Moon, "Evaluating Transformative Mediation in the U.S. Postal Service REDERESS Program" (2010) 27(3) *Conflict Resolution Quarterly* 257 ("*Nabatchi et al.*") at 258.
10. *Lee & Teh*, see above note 3 at 13.
11. *Bush & Folger*, see above note 6 at 49–51.
12. Ibid at 84.
13. *Bush & Folger*, see above note 6 at 89.
14. Charlie Irvine, "Transformative Mediation: A Critique" (2007) *Dispute Resolution and Negotiation e-Journal* at 9–10.
15. Nadja Alexander, "The Mediation Meta-model: The Realities of Mediation Practice" (2011) 12(6) *ADR Bulletin* 126 ("*Alexander*").
16. *Nabatchi et al.*, see above note 9 at 262.
17. *Bush & Folger*, see above note 6 at 165.
18. Ibid. at 154.
19. Robert A. Baruch Bush & Joseph P. Folger, "Transformative Mediation and Third Party Intervention: Ten Hallmarks of Transformative Approach to Practise" (1996) 13(4) *Mediation Quarter* 263 ("*Transformative Mediation*") at 271.
20. *Bush & Folger*, see above note 6 at 144.
21. Bernard S. Mayer, *Beyond Neutrality: Confronting the Crisis in Conflict Resolution* (Jossey-Bass, 2004) ("*Mayer*") at 133.
22. Ruth Charlton & Micheline Dewdney, *The Mediator's Handbook: Skills and Strategies for Practitioners* (Thomson Reuters, 2014) at 68.
23. Robert A. Creo, (2016). "Embracing and Using Anger in Mediation" (2016) 34(11) *Alternatives to the High Cost of Litigation* 166.

24. Cheryl Picard & Janet Siltanen, "Exploring the Significance of Emotion for Mediation Practice" (2013) 31(1) *Conflict Resolution Quarterly* 31.
25. *Transformative Mediation*, see above note 19 at 272.
26. Sudaresh Menon CJ, "Building Sustainable Mediation Programmes: A Singapore Perspective" (14 February 2015) at 3.
27. *Bush* & Folger see above note 6 at 214.
28. *Yang*, see above note 5 at 72.
29. *Transformative Mediation*, see above note 19 at 275.
30. Lisa Blomgren Amsler. "Transformative Mediation at the United States Postal Service" (2012) 5(4) *Negotiation and Conflict Management Research 354.*
31. *Mayer*, see above note *21* at 125–129.
32. *Supra* note 19 at 266.
33. Laurence Boulle, *Mediation Principles: Process and Practice* (LexisNexis, 2nd Edition, 2005) at 302.
34. *Lee & Teh*, see above note 3 at 62.
35. *Transformative Mediation*, see above note 19 at 268.
36. Ibid.
37. *Lee & Teh*, see above note 3 at 59.
38. Ibid. at 72.
39. Ibid. at 164.
40. Ibid. at 166.
41. Ibid. at 62.
42. *Skalstad,* see above note 7.
43. *Supra note 8* at 624.
44. Nadja Alexander, Joel Lee & Lum Kit-Wye, *Singapore Mediation Handbook* (LexisNexis, 2019) at 129.
45. *Alexander*, see above note 15 at 5.
46. *Nabatchi et al.*, see above note 9 at 282.

Chapter 11 "Paiseh!" — Apologies, Restorative Justice and Criminal Mediation in Singapore

1. This is a commonly used Singlish phrase, from the Hokkien dialect, often utilised to express one's sense of shame. For instance, see "11 unspoken rules of living in Singapore that only make sense to locals", *The Smart Local Singapore* <https://thesmartlocal.com/read/unspoken-rules/> (accessed 1 April 2020).

2. Tessa Wong, "The rise of Singlish", *British Broadcasting Corporation* (6 August 2015) <https://www.bbc.com/news/magazine-33809914> (accessed 2 April 2020).
3. Tan Ying Ying, "Commentary: Singlish is not English. That's not a bad thing.", *Channel News Asia* (19 May 2019) <https://www.channelnewsasia.com/news/commentary/singlish-singapore-english-language-code-switch-uneducated-11477190> (accessed 14 March 2020).
4. Karen Mira, "Is it good to let your kids fight their own battles?", *The Asian Parent Singapore* <https://sg.theasianparent.com/is-it-good-to-let-your-kids-fight-their-own-battles> (accessed 11 March 2020).
5. Lydia Lam, "Man initiated fight after staring incident on train, gets fine", *Channel News Asia* (25 November 2019) <https://www.channelnewsasia.com/news/singapore/man-initiated-fight-after-staring-incident-on-train-gets-fine-12122980> (accessed 10 March 2020).
6. For instance, see Donna L. Pavlick, "Apology and Mediation: The Horse and Carriage of the Twenty-First Century" (2003) 18 *Ohio State Journal on Dispute Resolution* 829 ("*Pavlick*") at 829.
7. For instance, see Barry R. Schlenker & Bruce W. Darby, "The Use of Apologies in Social Predicaments" (1981) 44(3) *Social Psychology Quarterly* 271.
8. For instance, see Carl D. Schneider, "What It Means to be Sorry: The Power of Apology in Mediation" (2000) 17 *Mediation Quarterly* 265 ("*Schneider*").
9. Eugene Teo & Carrie Chan, "Criminal Mediation in Singapore — Tailoring the Process to the Parties" (2017) *Asian Journal on Mediation* 68 ("*Teo and Chan*") at 68.
10. Istvan Lakatos, "Thoughts on Universalism versus Cultural Relativism, with Special Attention to Women's Rights" (2018) I *Pecs Journal of International and European Law* 6 at 10–14.
11. Joel Lee, "Culture and its Importance in Mediation" in Danny McFadden & George Lim SC, eds., *Mediation in Singapore — A Practical Guide* (Thomson Reuters, 2015) at 165.
12. Maryam H Rozlan, "Promoting ASEAN as a Platform for Collaborative Dispute Settlement — Institutionalising Administered Mediation in ASEAN" in Joel Lee & Marcus Lim, eds., *Contemporary Issues in Mediation Volume 2* (World Scientific, 2017) at 66–69.
13. For instance, see Lois Presser & Cynthia A Hamilton, "The Micropolitics of Victim-Offender Mediation" (2006) 76(3) *Sociological Inquiry* 316 at 337–338.

14. See Kee Oon, "Criminal Case Resolution" (2013) *Asian Journal on Mediation* 76 at [5], where the author recognized that Criminal Mediation means "different things in different jurisdictions", including differing approaches to mediation — particularly along the facilitative-evaluative divide.
15. For instance, see Rathna N. Koman, "Balancing the Force in Criminal Mediation" (2016) *Beijing Law Review* 171 ("*Koman*"), where the author equates the Criminal Case Resolution system with Criminal Mediation, although these terms refer to two different processes.
16. *Teo and Chan* see above note 9 at 68.
17. For instance, see Selina Lum, "Plea bargaining, Singapore-style", *The Straits Times* (15 March 2017), which provided a brief overview on the process of plea bargaining in Singapore.
18. For instance, see K C Vijayan, "More criminal cases going for mediation", *The Straits Times* (26 December 2013), which covered various practitioners' opinions on the CCR system.
19. For more detailed information about the CCR system, see, *inter alia*, Kessler Soh, "Criminal Case Resolution (CCR) in the Subordinate Courts of Singapore", *Australasian Institute of Judicial Administration Criminal Justice in Australia and New Zealand — Issues and Challenges for Judicial Administration Conference 2011* <https://aija.org.au/wpcontent/uploads/2017/08/Soh.pdf> (accessed 10 March 2020).
20. *Teo and Chan* see above note 9 at 69, see footnote 5.
21. *Koman*, see above note 15 at 172.
22. This has seen great success in Singapore. For instance, see former Chief Justice Chan Sek Keong's keynote address in the State Courts Workplan 2011, where His Honour shared that since the pilot CCR began in 2010, 60 judge days were saved.
23. For further details, see Nadja Alexander, Joel Lee & Lum Kit-Wye, *Singapore Mediation Handbook* (LexisNexis, 2019) ("*Alexander et al.*") at 349–350.
24. Laura Lau & Carrie Chan, "Mediation of Criminal Matters in the State Courts", in Danny McFadden & George Lim SC, eds., *Mediation in Singapore — A Practical Guide* (Thomson Reuters, 2017) ("*Lau & Chan*") at 407.
25. *Teo and Chan* see above note 9 at 70.
26. Criminal Procedure Code, Cap 68 (Rev Ed 2012) ("*CPC*"), Sections 151–153.

27. Community Mediation Centres Act, Cap 49A (Rev Ed 1998) ("*CMCA*") Section 15.
28. Constitution of the Republic of Singapore (1999 Reprint) Art 35(8).
29. Attorney-General's Chambers website <https://www.agc.gov.sg/our-roles/public-prosecutor/public-prosecutor-overview-of-functions> (accessed 12 March 2020).
30. *Lau &* Chan see above note 24.
31. Mark S. Umbreit, Robert B. Coates & Betty Vos, "The Impact of Victim-Offender Mediation: Two Decades of Research" (2000–2001) 5 *Fed Probation* 29.
32. Kimberly N. Grant, "Ten Dollars for Twenty-Four Years: Providing Justice for Exonerees Using Victim-Offender Mediation" (2008–2009) 15 *Dispute Resolution Magazine* at 19–21.
33. Josephine Kang & Dorcas Quek, "Mediation of Criminal Matters in the State Courts" in Danny McFadden & George Lim SC, eds., *Mediation in Singapore — A Practical Guide* (Thomson Reuters, 2017) ("*Kang & Quek*") at 364.
34. State Courts of Singapore, *Guide on Best Practices for Court Mediation.*
35. *Kang & Quek*, see above note 33 at 367.
36. *Schneider*, see above note 8 at 266.
37. Ibid.
38. Jeffrie G. Murphy & Jean Hampton, *Forgiveness and Mercy* (Cambridge University Press, 1988) ("*Murphy & Hampton*") at 28.
39. Peter J. Boyer, "The People's Network", *New Yorker* (3 August 1988) ("*Boyer*") at 28.
40. Erving Goffman, *Relations in Public: Microstudies of the Public Order* (Basic Books, 1971) ("*Goffman*").
41. Nicholas Tavuchis, *Mea Culpa: A Sociology of Apology and Reconciliation* (Stanford University Press, 1991) ("*Tavuchis*") at 13.
42. Olivia B. Waxman & Merrill Fabry, "From an Anonymous Tip to an Impeachment: A Timeline of Key Moments in the Clinton-Lewinsky Scandal", *Time* (4 May 2018) <https://time.com/5120561/bill-clinton-monica-lewinsky-timeline/> (accessed 20 March 2020).
43. Mary McGrory, "A Sorry Confession", *Washington Post* (20 August 1998) at A3.
44. Elizabeth Hyde, "The Power of Apology in Family Mediation", *Riverdale Mediation* (5 December 2011), <https://www.riverdalemediation.com/wp-

content/uploads/2019/03/E.-Hyde-The-power-of-apologies-in-family-mediation.pdf> (accessed 16 March 2020).

45. *Schneider*, see above note 8 at 267.
46. *Pavlick*, see above note 6 at 841 onwards.
47. *Lau* & Chan, see above note 24.
48. *CPC*, see above note 26 at Section 151(2)(a).
49. *CPC*, see above note 26 at Section 152(1).
50. Mandeep K. Dhami, "Offer and Acceptance of Apology in Victim-Offender Mediation" (2012) 20 *Critical Criminology* 45 at 46–48.
51. For instance, see D. Michelle Irwin & Shirley G. Moore, "The Young Child's Understanding of Social Justice" (1971) 5(3) *Developmental Psychology* 406 at 409–411.
52. *Tavuchis*, see above note 41.
53. Aaron Lazare, "Go Ahead, Say You're Sorry", *Psychology Today* (January-February 1995) at 40–42.
54. Paul Lauritzen, "Forgiveness: Moral Prerogative or Religious Duty?" (1987) 15(2) *The Journal of Religious Ethics* 141 at 145.
55. *Goffman*, see above note 40.
56. Jung Jin Choi, Diane L. Green & Stephen A. Kapp, "Victimization, Victims' Needs, and Empowerment in Victim-Offender Mediation" (2010) 17(3) *International Review of Victimology* 267 at 271–272.
57. Jonathan Cohen, "Advising Clients to Apologize" (1999) 72 *Southern California Law Review* 1009 ("*Cohen*") at 1021.
58. *Goffman*, see above note 40.
59. Deborah Tannen, "Contrite Makes Right", *Civilization* (April–May 1999) ("*Tannen*") at 69.
60. Hiroshi Wagatsuma & Arthur Rosett, "The Implications of Apology: Law and Culture in Japan and the United States" (1986) 20 *Law & Society Review* 461 at 476.
61. Ken-ichi Obuchi, Masuyo Kameda & Nariyuyki Adarie, "Apology as Aggression Control: Its Role in Mediating Appraisal of and Response to Harm" (1989) 56(2) *Journal of Personality & Social Psychology* 219 at 219–220.
62. *Pavlick*, see above note 6 at 845–846.
63. *Tannen*, see above note 59 at 67–69.
64. Deborah L. Levi, "The Role of Apology in Mediation" (1997) 72 *NYU Law Review* 1165 ("*Levi*") at 1203.
65. *Kang & Quek*, see above note 33 at 361.
66. *Pavlick*, see above note 6 at 846–847.

67. Patrick M. Gerkin, "Who Owns this Conflict? The Challenge of Community Involvement in Restorative Justice" (2012) 15 *Community Justice Review* 277 ("*Gerkin*") at 279–284.
68. *Cohen*, see above note 57 at 1012.
69. *Pavlick*, see above note 6 at 847–855.
70. *Schneider*, see above note 8 at 266.
71. Cheng Chi-Ying, "The effects of cosmopolitan culture, competitiveness, and need for cognitive closure on creativity" (2015) *Research Collection School of Social Sciences Paper 2035 at 2–3.*
72. Michael Frese, "Kiasu 2.0, or how to learn to love failure" *The Straits Times* (13 November 2017) <https://www.straitstimes.com/opinion/kiasu-20-or-how-to-learn-to-love-failure> (accessed 19 March 2020).
73. For instance, see Louisa Tang, "The Big Read: The Internet never forgets — ex-offenders struggle for redemption in the digital age", *Channel News Asia* (2 July 2019) <https://www.channelnewsasia.com/news/singapore/ex-offenders-internet-never-forgets-criminal-record-jobs-employ-11676726> (accessed 18 March 2020).
74. *Pavlick*, see above note 6 at 852–853.
75. Ng Wan Qing, "Could Power Imbalance be Power in Balance? Looking at Power Imbalances through a Singaporean Cultural Lens" in Joel Lee & Marcus Lim, eds., *Contemporary Issues in Mediation* Volume 1 (World Scientific, 2016) at 3–7.
76. For instance, see Anonymous, "What Nimbyism says about society" *The Straits Times* (14 January 2015) <https://www.straitstimes.com/opinion/what-nimbyism-says-about-society> (accessed 20 March 2020).
77. *Murphy* & Hampton, see above note 38.
78. *Boyer*, see above note 39.
79. *Schneider*, see above note 8 at 266–267.
80. *Lau & Chan*, see above note 24.
81. Olwen Bedford & Sheryl H. Chua, "Everything Also I Want: An Exploratory Study of Singapore *Kiasuism* (Fear of Losing Out)" (2018) 24(4) *Culture & Psychology* 491 at 491–495.
82. *Alexander et al.*, see above note 23 at 74–77.
83. *Gerkin*, see above note 67 at 278.
84. Justin Low Ching Wei, "Mandatory Mediation in Singapore: Cultural Compatibilities" in Joel Lee & Marcus Lim, eds., *Contemporary Issues in Mediation Volume 2* (World Scientific, 2017) ("*Low*") at 39–41.
85. *CMCA*, see above note 27 at Section 15(1).

86. For instance, see CPC Section 153(4), under which the Magistrate may consider the Respondent's failure to attend mediation sessions without reasonable grounds, when issuing further directions or during sentencing.
87. *Low*, see above note 84, at 38–42.
88. Harry C. Triandis, Robert Bontempo, Marcelo J. Villareal, Masaaki Asai & Nydia Lucca, "Individualism and Collectivism: Cross-Cultural Perspectives on Self-Ingroup Relationships" (1988) 54(2) *Journal of Personality and Social Psychology* 323 at 326.
89. Peter Rehm & Denise R. Beatty, "Legal Consequences of Apologizing" (1996) *Journal of Dispute Resolution* 115 at 115.
90. *Alexander et al.* see above note 23 at 77–79.
91. Ibid. at 71–74.
92. Selina Lum, "A less adversarial system that advances public interest", *The Straits Times* (9 November 2017) <https://www.straitstimes.com/opinion/a-less-adversarial-system-that-advances-public-interest> (accessed 22 March 2020).
93. Juliana Chan, "Turning disputes into win-win relationships", *Research @ Singapore Management University* (9 April 2018) <https://research.smu.edu.sg/news/smuresearch/2018/apr/02/turning-disputes-win-win-relationships> (accessed 22 March 2020).
94. *Teo and Chan*, see above note 9 at 76–77.
95. Casandra Wong, "Top values of Singapore society include '*kiasu*', 'complaining', 'self-centred': survey", *Yahoo! News* (30 July 2018) <https://sg.news.yahoo.com/top-values-singapore-society-include-kiasu-complaining-self-centred-survey-093021416.html> (accessed 1 April 2020).
96. Brian Poh, "Commentary: A hyper-competitive culture is breeding severe test anxiety among many students", *Channel News Asia* (29 September 2018) <https://www.channelnewsasia.com/news/commentary/hyper-competitive-culture-breeding-severe-test-anxiety-among-10744150> (accessed 22 March 2020).
97. Singapore After-Care Association, "What Happens After Graduation: The Challenges Faced by Ex-offenders and Support Required in Their Reintegration Post-graduation" <https://www.saca.org.sg/resources/ck/files/research/What%20Happens%20After%20Graduation%20-%20The%20Challenges%20Faced%20by%20Ex-offenders%20and%20Support%20Needed%20Post-graduation.pdf> (accessed 24 March 2020) at 11–15.

98. Charlene Tan, "'Our Shared Values' in Singapore: A Confucian Perspective" (2012) 62(4) *Educational Theory* 449 at 450–454.
99. *Lau & Chan*, see above note 24.
100. Telephone Interview with David Hoffman, Mediator, Hill & Barlow (13 November 1996), cited by *Levi*, see above note 64.
101. Mandeep K. Dhami, "Effects of a Victim's Response to an Offender's Apology: When the Victim Becomes the Bad Guy" (2016) 46(1) *European Journal of Social Psychology* 110 at 110–113.
102. For instance, see Jung Jin Choi & Margaret Severson, ""What! What kind of apology is this?": The nature of apology in victim offender mediation" (2009) 31(7) *Children and Youth Services Review* 813.
103. Ibid. at 817–819.
104. Douglas Stone, Bruce Patton, Sheila Heen & Roger Fisher, *Difficult Conversations: How to Discuss What Matters Most* (Penguin, 2010), cited by *Teo & Chan*, see above note 9.
105. Chan Min Hui, "Good Faith Participation in Mediation", in Joel Lee & Marcus Lim, eds., *Contemporary Issues in Mediation Volume 1* (World Scientific, 2016) at 128–131.
106. Aloysius Goh, "Features of a Dispute Suitable for Mediation" in Danny McFadden & George Lim SC, eds., *Mediation in Singapore — A Practical Guide* (Thomson Reuters, 2015) at 388.

www.ingramcontent.com/pod-product-compliance
Lightning Source LLC
LaVergne TN
LVHW011815200926
848484LV00005B/1210
* 9 7 8 9 8 1 1 2 4 1 4 2 0 *